JUICING & smoothies

Maria Costantino

JUICING &
smoothies

Published by SILVERDALE BOOKS
An imprint of Bookmart Ltd
Registered number 2372865
Trading as Bookmart Ltd
Blaby Road
Wigston
Leicester LE18 4SE

© 2006 D&S Books Ltd

D&S Books Ltd
Kerswell,
Parkham Ash, Bideford
Devon, England
EX39 5PR

e-mail us at:- enquiries@d-sbooks.co.uk

This edition printed 2006

ISBN 1-84509-278-3

DS0097. Smoothies & Juicing

Creative Director: Sarah King
Editor: Debbie Key
Project editor: Nicky Barber
Designer: Debbie Fisher
Photographer: Paul Forrester

Fonts: Avant Garde, Gill Sans, Hammer

Printed in Thailand

5 7 9 10 8 6 4

contents

Introduction
Smoothies for Health and Vitality!

Smoothies originated on the California beaches where warm weather and cool, healthy drinks are part of the lifestyle. When blenders were introduced, thirsty surfers, skaters and anyone else who happened along could buy delicious, refreshing drinks made with fresh California orange juice, bananas and berries – with or without ice. The thick, luscious texture of these drinks led to them being called smoothies and soon new flavour combinations were being introduced, along with ice cream and healthy yoghurt.

Smoothies can be made from fruit or vegetables, or a mix of the two, as long as there is a liquid base. They can be served cold or, in the case of vegetable smoothies, hot like a soup. Because they are blended and thickly textured it's easy to incorporate herbs, spices, seeds (such as sesame, sunflower and flax), grains and flakes (such as rice, oats and barley) and nuts into the recipes.

Smoothies in your diet

For decades, our parents and health practitioners have been telling us to eat more fruit and vegetables and to cut down on the fatty, sugary, salty and highly processed foods that have become part of our culture of eating in the West.

We know we should 'eat five' (portions of fruit and vegetables) each day, but most of us don't. Instead, we undermine the value of our food by eating too much of the wrong kinds and too little of the right kinds. In the USA, for example, the average adult manages just one-and-a-half portions of fruit and vegetables a day; while in Britain a remarkable 65% of the population eat only one portion per day! No wonder we moan about being tired, run down, sick and lacking in 'joie de vivre'!

The recipes in this book are simple, quick, relatively inexpensive and effective ways of making sure you get at least some of the goodness from those 'five a day'.

To Juice or Not to Juice?

While fruit and vegetable juices are often the basis of smoothies, the overwhelming majority of recipes in this book don't require a fancy juice extractor.

Juicing machines may be a good idea but they have one serious drawback: while they provide juice from all sorts of produce, it's juice and nothing but the juice! There's no insoluble fibre – it's left behind in the machine. Using a blender and 'pulping' the whole fruit means you get the juice and the fibre in a thicker purée.

It's true, some things are easier to juice than others: everyone knows how to squeeze an orange, a lemon, a lime or a grapefruit! But what about an apple? A kiwi? A raspberry? The answer is to send them all for a spin in the blender. You won't get a thin juice like you would in a carton, but a thicker 'purée' that's packed with flavour, vitamins, minerals and fibre. If a fruit mix is too thick for your taste, just thin it down a little with a splash of water.

Ready-made juices

There is no 'smoothie secret police' that watches you to make sure you don't buy fruit or vegetable juices from your supermarket! It really is OK to use ready-made juices – but do check the labels carefully. Freshly squeezed or juiced fruit and vegetable products will be in the chiller cabinet as they don't have any added preservatives and therefore have a short 'shelf-life'. Pure juices are not based on juice concentrates – these are evaporated and then re-diluted, a process in which they can lose many of their essential nutrients as well as some of their flavour and aroma.

Canned fruit and frozen fruit work too!

Smoothies are colder, thicker and smoother when they are made from frozen fruits or vegetables. One of the most economical ways of enjoying fruits out of season is to bulk buy when they are around and freeze them! Peaches, plums, berries, apple slices, melon balls, you name them, you can freeze them! Canned fruit, too, should never be overlooked: modern canning methods mean that, in most cases, the nutrient levels are comparable with fresh fruit or vegetables. But, as with fresh fruit, it's always best to buy organically grown produce and produce packed in its own juice, water or (in the case of fruit) apple juice with no added sugar or salt.

Cooked and canned vegetables

Spinach juice? And just how do you get a carrot to give up its juice without a juice extractor? Well, it's actually quite easy: just remember that the main content of fruit and vegetables is water in varying amounts! Cooking softens the taste and texture of vegetables, often making them more palatable. Hard root vegetables such as carrots, beetroots and potatoes must be cooked before you can use them in smoothies because they cannot be liquified in their raw state in ordinary blenders. Some 'stringy' or fibrous vegetables such as celery and leeks can also be

cooked – try steaming them! Alternatively, after blending, raw vegetable smoothies can be heated into soup until the veggies are tender!

If all this sounds like hard work then don't despair. You CAN use canned vegetables! The nutrient value is comparable to that of fresh, cooked vegetables and now the range of organic foods is increasing, you can get organic veggies in cans too. In all the vegetable smoothie recipes, canned and fresh veggies are interchangeable:

Use one 398ml (14fl oz) can for each 250ml (9fl oz) of chopped fresh veggies. If you use the liquid in the can as well, you can reduce the amount of other liquid in the recipe by about 3 tablespoons.

Smoothies are for now!

Smoothies are best enjoyed straight away – as soon as they've been made! Once 'liquid', many fruits and vegetables begin to oxidise quickly and mixtures of different densities will start to separate and they'll look and taste pretty awful.

Hey, Big Blender!

As I mentioned earlier, you don't need a juice extractor for the recipes in this book. Having said that, take a look at your blender or food processor and the instruction booklet that came with it. You may be surprised to find that your machine already has a special blade or attachment for dealing with extracting juice from some fruits and vegetables.

Make sure your blender is strong enough to deal with ice cubes and frozen fruit – the instruction manual will tell you!

Most blenders have at least three settings: off, slow and fast. Start blending smoothies on a slow speed and then move up to fast to whizz them into a frenzy.

In addition to your blender, most of the gadgets and gizmos you need are probably already in your kitchen cupboards.

Weighing scales and measuring spoons are useful for when you need to keep an eye on quantities. Because of the differences between metric and imperial weights and measures, to say nothing of American cups and sticks, the measurements given in the recipes are approximate equivalents. If you find you've got more, or less, than the quantity required in the recipe, who cares! You can alter any of the recipes to suit your taste!

Chopping board: some fruit and vegetables will have to be chopped up to fit into your blender – there's no way you'll get a whole pineapple a blender!

Knives/peelers are already in your kitchen. Fruits and veggies need to be peeled before use – especially non-organic produce – and some, like the lovely kiwi, may cause allergic reactions. Where there is a possible risk of allergic reaction, this is indicated in the section on 'food facts'.

Glasses: whatever you do, don't take slugs of smoothies direct from the blender jug! Apart from dribbling it down your chest, you'll end up transferring some of your body's primary digestive enzyme – saliva – into the juice and it will start digesting it in the jug! A large part of the satisfaction we get from dining out is from the 'look' of food: get the same satisfaction at home by using an attractive glass for your smoothies and take a moment to demonstrate your artistry with a decorative garnish too.

A simple slice of lemon, orange, or kiwi, a sprig of mint or lemon balm, a sprinkling of herbs, or a bunch of fresh leaves will please the eye and boost the appetite. Add a straw, a swizzle stick, or an edible swizzle stick in the form of a stick of cucumber, carrot or celery. One of the nicest surprises in a cool drink on a hot summer's day, is to discover that the ice cubes are made of apple or grape juice and that there are grapes, blueberries or strawberries frozen inside them!

When enough is enough

Remember, enjoy smoothies as part of a balanced diet. Clever as they are, smoothies alone cannot provide the complete range of nutritional needs for the body: we all need a balance of fats, carbohydrates and proteins for our bodies to function completely and to maintain health. While fruit smoothies are very tasty, it is important that we balance them with vegetable smoothies otherwise we would be consuming far too much sugar, which is present as fructose in all fruits.

Food Facts

The energy-boosting and medicinal properties of foods have been acknowledged for thousands of years and modern scientific research has found hundreds of beneficial nutrients in the foods we eat. By applying this knowledge of the nutrients available in the 'food pharmacy' and how they work, we can truly get the most out of what we eat.

Note: If you are ill, or if you have or suspect you may have an allergy or food intolerance, you need to consult a doctor. The recipes suggested are NOT substitutes for medical advice or prescribed medications.

Food Facts: Fruit

Citrus fruits

The main providers of Vitamin C, citrus fruits include oranges, lemons, limes, grapefruits, and mandarins – which also include tangerines, satsumas and clementines.

Warning! Some migraine sufferers may be sensitive to one or all citrus fruits. It is advisable to avoid oranges if you suffer from rheumatoid arthritis. If they are consumed in excess, all citrus fruits – especially lemons – can deplete the body's reserves, the bones and teeth, of calcium.

Oranges

Famed for their high Vitamin C content, oranges also contain potassium and some calcium. The pith is an exceptionally good source of bioflavinoids (Vitamin P) which strengthen the walls of the tiny blood capillaries. The peel contains hesperidin and limonene which are used in the treatment of chronic bronchitis.

Nutrients and active ingredients: Vitamins A, B6, C, thiamine, folic acid, magnesium, potassium, phosphorous, iron, riboflavin, protein, sugars

Beneficial properties: Antioxidant, anti-stress, lowers cholesterol, increases iron absorption

Lemons

One of the most effective remedies for treating colds and flu, as well as indigestion, lemons help protect the mucus membrane lining of the digestive tract and are said to be a stimulant for the liver and pancreas. Their antibacterial qualities make lemons a traditional choice for sore throats.

Nutrients and active ingredients: Vitamin C, some B vitamins, E, potassium, magnesium, calcium, phosphorous, copper, zinc, iron, manganese, bioflavinoids, limonene and mucilage.

Beneficial properties: Antibacterial, antioxidant, antiallergic. Lower blood-fat levels and help to maintain the health of the heart, nerves and muscle tissue.

Limes

While limes have more vitamin C than a grapefruit, they have less than an orange or lemon.

Nutrients and active ingredients: Vitamin C, folate, calcium, potassium, citric acid, fibre, bioflavinoids

Beneficial properties: Antioxidant, antibacterial

Grapefruits

The largest member of the citrus family, pink grapefruits are higher in Vitamin C than white ones. A popular 'slimmer's food', grapefruit is an 'eliminator', a powerful detoxer, stimulating the liver.

Nutrients and active ingredients: Vitamins A, C, folate, potassium, bioflavinoids, citric and phenolic acids, fibre, pectin, sugars

Beneficial properties: Antioxidant, anticancer, antimicrobial, lowers blood pressure, lowers cholesterol, stimulates the digestive system, stimulates the immune system, detoxing

Mandarins

Mandarins – of which the satsuma, the Mediterranean mandarin and the common mandarin are the main hybrids – are less acidic than grapefruits or lemons, but still good sources of Vitamin C and folate, although they do contain less potassium and fewer of the B vitamins.

Nutrients and active ingredients: Vitamin C, B1 (thiamine), potassium, folate

Beneficial properties: Antioxidant, anticancer, lowers cholesterol, circulation improvers, good for sore throats

Pome fruits

Pome fruits include apples, pears and quinces.

Apples

Traditionally apples have been used for treating stomach upsets and their soluble fibre is a vital weapon in relieving constipation. The sugar in apples is mostly fructose which is broken down and releases its energy slowly: this helps to keep blood sugar levels on an even keel.

Nutrients and active ingredients: Vitamin C, potassium, malic acid, tannin, fibre, pectin, sugars

Beneficial properties: Lowers cholesterol, lowers blood pressure, detoxifying, aids the digestive system

Pears

Ripe pears are a good source of soluble pectin which is a bowel regulator, and they don't just lower cholesterol, they actually eliminate it from the body! A reasonable source of Vitamin C, they also have Vitamin A, potassium and a little Vitamin E, but it's their soluble fibre that is the real winner – a much tastier alternative to bran!

Nutrients and active ingredients: Vitamins C, A, E, potassium, fibre

Beneficial properties: Good for energy and recovery after illness, good for the digestive system; cholesterol-lowering

Warning! Fresh pears contain a sugar-based alcohol called sorbitol. This sugar-free sweetener is used in many 'tooth friendly' foods and toothpaste, but it may cause diarrhoea in some susceptible folk.

Stone fruits

Apricots

High in Vitamin A and containing several minerals, apricots are good sources of carbohydrates and are low in fat. In recipes calling for apricots, you can substitute nectarines or peaches, or even dried fruits, but 'rehydrate' them first either by soaking in cold water for an hour or cooking in a little water over a low heat until soft and plump. Then drain off the liquor and use the fruits as if fresh.

Nutrients and active ingredients: Vitamin A, carotene, B2, B3, B5, calcium, magnesium, potassium, copper, iron, zinc, fibre, sugar (Dried apricots are also a rich source of iron.)

Beneficial properties: Antioxidant; stimulate the immune system by encouraging antibody production; detoxifying; help stabilise blood sugars; help the release of energy from food and stored tissues; enhance the transport of oxygen in the blood.

Warning! Dried fruits that have been treated with sulphur dioxide should be avoided as they can trigger asthma attacks.

Peaches and nectarines

Nutritionally there is little between the nectarine and the 'Persian plum' or peach, whose botanical name is **persica** because early scientists believed it had originated in Persia and not, as we now know, in China.

Nutrients and active ingredients: Vitamin C, betacarotene, some fibre, folic acid, potassium, phosphorous

Beneficial properties: Antioxidant, good for the digestive system, gentle laxative, virtually fat and sodium free, ideal for those with high cholesterol and blood pressure problems, believed to benefit the nervous system and help prevent degenerative disease.

Cherries

Cherries are good detoxers and a mild laxative; they soothe the nervous system and can help relieve stress. But it is their content of ellagic acid which inhibits the growth of cancerous cells that makes these juicy little fruits valuable in the fight against cancers.

Nutrients and active ingredients: Vitamins C, A, bioflavinoids, ellagic acid, phosphorous, potassium and calcium plus minimal amounts of B-complex vitamins (B2, folic acid)

Beneficial properties: Antioxidant, anticancer, diuretic; low sodium, beneficial to the nervous system, stress-reliever; mild laxative.

Plums

Plums are widely used in Oriental medicine, especially Japanese Umiboshi, to treat digestive disorders.

Nutrients and active ingredients: A little Vitamin C, modest amounts of Vitamin A and some Vitamin E, folic acid, betacarotene. Good sources of potassium. When dried as prunes, they are excellent sources of iron, Vitamin A, potassium, calcium and magnesium.

Beneficial properties: Good for the heart and circulation, good for the digestive system (gently laxative, especially dried as prunes), diuretic

Warning! Dried plums (prunes) and all dried fruits that have been treated with sulphur dioxide should be avoided as this can trigger asthma attacks.

Avocados

The Vitamin E contained in avocados stimulates the production of collagen which helps smooth out wrinkles. It's also a high-protein, high-energy and high-protection factor food containing anti-fungal and antibacterial chemicals. The mono-unsaturated fats – especially oleic acid – make avocados one of the most powerful antioxidant foods known to man and offer protection against heart diseases, strokes and cancers. The B6 helps iron out mood swings, making avocados very useful for PMS sufferers.

Nutrients and active ingredients: Vitamins E, K, B1, B2, B3, B5, biotin, folate, potassium, zinc, carotenoids, fibre, unsaturated fatty acids including oleic acid

Beneficial properties: Anticancer, anti fungal, antioxidant

Warning! If you are allergic to natural rubber (latex) you have a 50-50 chance of being allergic to avocados.

Melons

Cooling and delicious in summer, all forms of melon are stimulating to the kidneys and gently laxative. Cantaloupe melons are particularly valuable in the 'food pharmacy' as they increase the release of energy from other foods and have a high level of carotenoids which may inhibit the growth of cancer cells.

Nutrients and active ingredients: Cantaloupe: Vitamins A, C, B3, carotenoids; watermelons: Vitamin B5

Beneficial properties: Cantaloupe: antioxidant, anticancer, laxative, diuretic, low sodium; watermelons: energy metabolizers, diuretic, laxative, low sodium

Grapes

Grapes contain far more aromatic compounds than any other fruit including astringent tannins, flavones, linanol, nerol and geraniol, which are believed to have anticancer properties.

Nutrients and active ingredients: Vitamins B3, B6, E, biotin, magnesium, phosphorous, copper, iron, selenium, zinc

Beneficial properties: anti-inflammatory, antioxidant, anticancer, detoxifying, diuretic

Warning! Since most grapes are sprayed during cultivation, careful washing is vital prior to ingestion.

Berry fruits

Hundreds of wild fruits are called berries but only about ten have been domesticated and cultivated. These are much larger than their wild cousins but are still packed wth vitamins and minerals.

Strawberries

Linneaus, the great Swedish botanist, recommended strawberries as a cure for arthritis, gout and rheumatism – chronic ailments from which he suffered. It seems that the berries help to eliminate uric acid from the body.

Nutrients and active ingredients: Vitamin C, B3, B5, iron, soluble fibre, pectin

Beneficial properties: Reputed to reduce high blood pressure, help in elimination of uric acid and kidney stones; help prevent and treat anaemia and fatigue, lower cholesterol, anti-viral properties, astringent, diuretic and mildly laxative

Warning! Some people may be sensitive to strawberries and have allergic reactions, which in some instances may be extreme, and even life-threatening.

Blueberries

Blueberries have a fair amount of Vitamin C and small amounts of B1, betacarotene and potassium, but it is their antibacterial anthocyanosides which are valued in strengthening the walls of blood vessels, and in the treatment of cystitis and other urinary infections.

Nutrients and active ingredients: Vitamin C, B1, betacarotene, potassium, anthocyanosides, fibre

Beneficial properties: antibacterial, antioxidant, antiseptic, anti-inflammatory, toning effect on the blood vessels

Blackberries

High in both vitamins C and E, blackberries are valuable antioxidants protecting against diseases and infections.

Nutrients and active ingredients: Vitamin C, E, B3, folate, manganese, iron, potassium, citric acid, soluble fibre

Beneficial properties: Antioxidant, toning, good for the heart, circulation and the skin, good for colds and flu recovery

Raspberries

The nutrients in raspberries make them ideal foods for convalescents as well as those with heart problems, fatigue, and depression. A high Vitamin C content means that for 100g (4oz) you'll get 75% of your recommended daily allowance.

Nutrients and active ingredients: Vitamin C, B3, biotin, folate, manganese, iron, citric acid, fibre

Beneficial properties: Antioxidant, detoxifying, toning: good for gum disease, upset stomachs and diarrhoea

Blackcurrants

An exceptionally rich source of Vitamin C, blackcurrants are valuable also for their anthocyanosides – the pigments in their purple-black skin – which are antibacterial and anti-inflammatory.

Nutrients and active ingredients: Vitamin C, anthocyanosides, potassium

Beneficial properties: anti-inflammatory, antibacterial, immune boosting; good for recovery from colds and flu, anticancer, diuretic, stress-buster, helps lower blood pressure

Cranberries

Thanks to the high Vitamin C content of cranberries, early European settlers in North America were able to avoid the terrors of scurvy. The most popular 'medicinal' use of the berries today is in the treatment and prevention of cystitis: the juice prevents the bacteria from sticking to the bladder wall.

Nutrients and active ingredients: Vitamin C, iron, anthocyanosides, benzoic, citric and quinic acids, fibre

Beneficial properties: immune boosting; antibacterial, good for cystitis and urinary infections

Tropical and exotic fruits

Once the preserve of the very rich, today we are indeed fortunate that we can enjoy a huge variety of fruits that are not native to our own countries. Supermarkets, greengrocers and market stalls not only provide apples and oranges but persimmons, pomegranates and carambolas (star fruits) to serve the tastes of our multicultural communities.

Kiwi fruits

With twice as much vitamin C as an orange and more fibre than an apple, kiwis are rich in potassium as well – a lack of which can lead to high blood pressure, depression, chronic fatigue and poor digestion. They also contain an enzyme called actinidin, which has a similar action to the papain found in papaya.

Nutrients and active ingredients: Vitamins A, C, B3, fibre, potassium, actinidin

Beneficial properties: antioxidant, immune-boosting, good for the skin and digestive system, gentle laxative

Warning! Some people may be sensitive to the furry skin: avoid contact with the mouth.

Papayas (paw paws)

Full of Vitamin C and an excellent source of betacarotene which the body then converts into Vitamin A, papayas also contain the digestive enzyme papain.

Nutrients and active ingredients: Vitamin C, betacarotene, fibre, papain, potassium, phosphorous

Beneficial properties: antiallergic, antibacterial, antioxidant, detoxer, immune-boosting, good for the digestive system, beneficial for the skin and eyes

Mangoes

One mango will provide you with a day's Vitamin C, two-thirds of your Vitamin A, half your Vitamin E and a quarter of your fibre needs, a cocktail of potassium, iron and nictinic acid working as antioxidants, and papain, the protein-digesting enzyme.

Nutrients and active ingredients: Vitamins A, C, E, B3, potassium, iron, nictinic acid, papain, fibre

Beneficial properties: antibacterial, anticancer, antioxidant, energy-boosting, immune system booster, detoxer.

Warning! The peel of mangoes, especially when fully ripe, can be highly irritant. The fruit belongs to the same family as poison ivy and anyone sensitized by contact with this or mangoes may suffer a severe reaction. Even if you are not sensitive, it is advisable to wear gloves if you are preparing a lot of mangoes, as excessive handling can irritate the skin.

Passion fruit

You can eat passion fruit like a melon, purée it or turn it into juice. Whichever way you use them, they are delicious and boost your energy levels, lift your spirits and help ensure healthy skin and nerves.

Nutrients and active ingredients: Vitamins A, C, B2, B3, magnesium, phosphorous, iron, zinc, fibre

Beneficial properties: anti-allergy, anticancer, antioxidant, energy-boosting

Pineapple

Pineapple's most valuable ingredient is an enzyme called bromelain which can digest many times its own weight of protein and has been found to be valuable in breaking down blood clots.

Nutrients and active ingredients: Vitamin A, B-complex, C, calcium, magnesium, manganese, phosphorous, potassium, copper, iron, zinc, bromelain, fibre

Beneficial properties: anti-inflammatory, diuretic, lowers blood pressure, helps prevent blood clots, speeds up tissue repair, good for the digestive system, energy boosting

Note: In the canning process and commercial juicing process, some of the beneficial properties of pineapple are lost. If using canned fruit, use pineapple canned in natural juice, not in heavy sugar-syrup.

Bananas

With a high sugar content, bananas are excellent energy boosters and, except for raspberries, are richer in minerals than any other fruit. The fibre is soluble which helps lower cholesterol, the potassium helps beat cramp and the B6 can help alleviate the worst effects of PMS.

Nutrients and active ingredients: Vitamins C, B3, B5, B6, biotin, magnesium, manganese, potassium, soluble fibre

Beneficial properties: stress-buster, energy-booster, stimulates the digestive system, lowers cholesterol, helps relieve cramps and symptoms of PMS

Dates

It is the mineral content of dates – especially their iron content – which is of interest to contemporary scientists. Of the 100 or so varieties, the dates we are most likely to find are Deglet Noors (from Algeria) and Medjools (from Morocco), although many more varieties are now grown in the USA.

Nutrients and active ingredients: Vitamin C (fresh only), Vitamin B-complex, folate iron (varies between variety), potassium, fibre

Beneficial properties: energy-boosters, help treat anaemia, used in treatments for ME, mildly laxative

Food Facts: Vegetables

Vegetables, like fruit, are nature's storehouses of goodness. Rich in vital vitamins and minerals, their health-giving properties have been known for hundreds of years and, more recently, have been the subject of scientific enquiry. Like fruits, some of the flavours are strong, while others are surprisingly sweet!

Wherever possible choose organically grown vegetables: commercially grown vegetables are grown using organo-phosphate pesticides which may leave a toxic residue. Wash all vegetables thoroughly prior to use.

Root vegetables

Carrots

The orange colour is the result of the betacarotene content: a single carrot has enough for your body to convert into a whole day's supply of Vitamin A – vital for healthy skin, night vision and the disease-resistant mucus membranes.

Nutrients and active ingredients: Vitamins A, C, E, K, folate, calcium, manganese, phosphorous, chromium, iron, zinc, betacarotene, fibre

Beneficial properties: anticancer; antioxidant, good for skin and eyes, good for the heart and circulation

Beetroot

Research is now beginning to explain how the deep, red colour of beetroot contains anti-carcinogens and how the vegetable encourages the body's cells to absorb increased amounts of oxygen. Its red colour has also made it useful in treating disorders of the blood such as anaemia and leukaemia.

Nutrients and active ingredients: folate, calcium, manganese, potassium, iron, betanin, malonic acid, phytosterol, saponin, protein, fibre

Beneficial properties: anticancer; anti-inflammatory, antioxidant, immune-boosting, boosts cell oxygenation, rejuvenating, detoxing

!Warning Don't panic if your stools or urine are bright red after eating beetroot! It's only the betanin, the natural colour of the vegetable, passing through!

Florence fennel

Although not a powerhouse of vitamins and minerals, fennel in the bulb form – the seeds have been used medicinally for thousands of years – has numerous volatile oils that impart a unique flavour.

Nutrients and active ingredients: Vitamin A, volatile oils including anisic acid, fenchone, limonine, anethole

Beneficial properties: diuretic, boosts the digestive system.

Onions and spring onions (scallions)

Onions belong to the same family as leeks, garlic, spring onions, chives and shallots. Like garlic, onions are currently undergoing extensive medical research which is fast confirming their reputation as a cure-all. They are especially effective on the circulatory system, helping to break down blood clots. Onions are also used to treat chest infections.

Nutrients and active ingredients: Vitamin C, B, C, calcium, magnesium, potassium, allinase

Beneficial properties: powerful diuretic, antibacterial

Leeks

The Romans believed that leeks were good for the throat, and Emperor Nero ate them every day to improve the quality of his voice! Leeks were a staple vegetable of medieval Europeans: the old Anglo-Saxon word 'leek' meant simply 'vegetable'.

Nutrients and active ingredients: Vitamin A, B complex, C, calcium, magnesium, folic acid, betacarotene (in green leaves), potassium

Beneficial properties: antibacterial, anticancer, diuretic, eliminate uric acid, reduce high blood pressure and cholesterol levels, good for sore throats

Garlic

The antibacterial properties of garlic were first proven scientifically by Louis Pasteur in 1858. The sulphur compound allicin which is released when garlic is crushed lowers cholesterol.

Nutrients and active ingredients: Vitamin B6, magnesium, phosphorous, potassium, iron, zinc, bioflavinoids, glucokinin, mucilage, phytohormones, volatile oils

Beneficial properties: antibacterial, anticoagulant, anticatarrhal, antioxidant, antiseptic, expectorant, detoxer, lowers blood pressure, lowers cholesterol

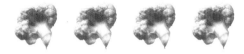

Brassicas

The brassica family – of which cabbage, cauliflower and brussels sprouts are the best known – is valued for Vitamin C and betacarotene and increasingly, its anticancer, properties.

Warning! People with sensitive skins should be careful when handling brassicas as they can cause contact dermatitis.

Warning! All members of the brassica family should be eaten only in modest amounts by people taking thyroid medication (thyroxine) or iodine for under active thyroids. Brassicas contain goitrogenic factors which interfere with the thyroid's ability to absorb iodine.

Cabbage: red, white and Savoy (dark green)

The anticancer properties of cabbage are attributed to the presence of phytochemicals such as glucosinolates, which as soon as the vegetable is chopped are released and converted into anti-carcinogenic indoles. The dark-green, leafy Savoy cabbage is the 'super cabbage', with a high Vitamin C content, folate, and betacarotene.

Nutrients and active ingredients: Vitamin C, A (Savoy), B3, folate, calcium, potassium, iron, sulphur compounds

Beneficial properties: anticancer, antioxidant, energy-boosting

Spinach

The large amounts of iron that are present in spinach are in fact not easily absorbed by the body because of the presence of oxalic acid. But spinach is an excellent source of chlorophyll which is beneficial to the blood and rich in folic acid.

Nutrients and active ingredients: Vitamins A, E, B2, B3, folate, calcium, iron, magnesium, manganese, potassium, zinc, carotenoids (lutein and zeaxanthin), chlorophyll, oxalic acid, fibre, protein

Beneficial properties: anticancer, antioxidant, anti-viral, immune-boosting, good for sight protection, energy-booster

Salad vegetables

Celery

Calming on the the nerves – especially the essential oils which are extracted from the seeds – celery has been shown to reduce high blood pressure. Traditionally it has been used to treat rheumatism and gout: its diuretic properties make it a useful detoxer and expeller of uric acid.

Nutrients and active ingredients: Vitamins A, C, B-complex, E, calcium, magnesium, phosphorous, potassium, sodium

Beneficial properties: reduces high blood pressure, calmative, diuretic, detoxer

Cucumbers

While they are more than 95% water, cucumbers also have some Vitamin A and potassium and are amazingly high in Vitamin E – which is effective as a skin treatment.

Nutrients and active ingredients: Vitamins A (with skin intact), E, potassium

Beneficial properties: detoxer, therapeutic for the skin and eyes, mildly diuretic, refreshing and cooling to the skin and intestines

Tomatoes

Although thousands of varieties are known, a mere five hundred varieties are available in a range of sizes, shapes and colours including white, striped, orange, bell, vase-shaped and round!

Nutrients and active ingredients: Vitamins A, C, B3, E, carotenoids, potassium, low sodium

Beneficial properties: anticancer, antioxidant, anti-viral, immune-boosting, energy-boosting

Warning! Tomatoes are members of the *Solanaceae* family and may aggravate the pain and discomfort of rheumatoid arthritis. They are also not recommended for those suffering from persistent mouth ulcers or eczema.

Watercress

The benzyl mustard oil which gives watercress is 'bite' is also a powerful antibiotic, but doesn't harm the levels of flora in the gut.

Nutrients and active ingredients: Vitamins A, C, E, B3, B6, calcium, manganese, iron, glucoinolates, volatile oil, iodine, protein, fibre

Beneficial properties: anticancer, antioxidant, anti-scorbutic, antibiotic, purgative, expectorant

Peppers: red, green and yellow

Sweet peppers (such as pimentos and chilli peppers) are members of the **capsicum** genus of the **Solanaceae** family which also includes tomatoes. An important source of nutrients, Vitamins C, A and folic acid, they are also low in calories.

Nutrients and active ingredients: Vitamins A, C, B6, carotenoids, fibre

Beneficial properties: antioxidant, antiallergenic, anticancer, stress-busters, good for strengthening and maintaining eyesight

Warning! Peppers are members of the **Solanaceae** family, which includes deadly nightshade and tobacco, and may aggravate the pain and discomfort of rheumatoid arthritis.

Herbs and spices

The most ancient of Western herbals, **De Materia Medica** by Dioscorides dates from the first century AD, but the use of herbs and spices is as old as mankind itself and some of the greatest advances in medicine have origins in their study.

Parsley

Paresley contains a number of essential oils and is also rich in vitamins A and C, iron, calcium and potassium. Traditionally used as an anti-inflammatory, it is also a powerful antioxidant, diuretic and digestive aid.

Dill

Widely used in Scandinavian cookery, the lacey, feathery leafed dill takes its name from the Scandinavian word **dilla** which means to 'lull' because of its particularly calming effects on the digestive system, relieving flatulence and stomach pains.

Rosemary

Rosemary is a tonic and stimulant for the brain cortex. It contains vitamin A, calcium, magnesium, iron and zinc as well as volatile oils which make it an effective antioxidant and anti-inflammatory.

Thyme

Thymol, the major essential oil in thyme, is an ingredient in many commercial products, especially in antiseptics, toothpastes and mouthwashes because of its soothing effects on the smooth muscles of the tracheae (wind pipe).

Basil

Like rosemary, basil also has something of a reputation for improving the memory, so it can be helpful during times of mental exertion. It is also useful for treating headaches, indigestion and flatulence.

Mint

Pliny the Naturalist said mint had a scent that awakened the spirit – but it also stimulates the appetite. Mint has an interest property in that its smell has a warming effect on the body, which then becomes cooling and refreshing.

Lemon balm

The sweet-tasting herb has a calming effect on the nerves, lowers blood pressure and is also an antidepressant. A leaf rubbed on an insect sting or bite is a good way to soothe the skin.

Sage

Sage contains vitamin A, calcium, magnesium, manganese, potassium, zinc and volatile oils which make it antiseptic and anti-inflammatory. It is helpful in treating menstrual problems and PMS.
!Warning Sage can interfere with the production of breast milk, so don't overuse this herb when breast-feeding).

Coriander

Rich in minerals and volatile oils, coriander has long been used by Ayurvedic physicians as a diuretic. It is also antispasmodic – it eases abdominal cramps so it's good for digestive disturbances.

Nutmeg

It is the myriticin which is the 'active component' in nutmeg: its effects on the brain are similar to mescaline! Consequently it can be toxic in large doses. It stimulates the appetite, and is good if you are feeling a little queasy.

Cinnamon

The volatile oil which contains cinnamaldehyde is a mild painkiller and also helps to lower raised blood pressure.

Ginger

Ginger is a warming and comforting remedy for travel sickness and morning sickness as well as colds and chills because it stimulates peripheral circulation and helps the body rid itself of toxins. (Dried ginger is much more pungent than the fresh root: a pinch to ¼ teaspoon of dried ginger is generally enough to satisfy most tastes.)

Milk & Dairy Alternatives

Nutritionally, milk is a very valuable source of vitamins and minerals, especially for children, adolescents and during pregnancy: it contains Vitamins A,D, E, calcium, protein, zinc. B2 (riboflavin) and B12. It is also relatively inexpensive, widely available, and easily consumed. Roughly one-third of the average adult's daily protein requirement can be met with 500 ml (1 pint) of milk along with 15% of our energy needs.

But there are drawbacks. Milk has a high fat content, and although the fat content is reduced when the milk is skimmed or semi skimmed, so are the vitamins. This is why semi-skinned and skimmed milk should not be given to the under-fives.

For those with allergies – such as eczema and asthma – which can be triggered by cow's milk, there are alternatives: goat's milk, ewe's milk, soya milk and rice milk.

Soya milk and tofu

Soya beans contain the most complete protein and lend themselves to a whole range of highly nutritious products from tofu (bean curd) and soy sauce, to soya milk, cheese and yoghurt. But it is the anticancer properties of soya that has attracted much of the attention in recent years: its antioxidant content protects

against free radicals which can lead to heart and circulatory disease as well as to cancer.

Tofu is a curd made from soya beans that is high in Vitamin B, potassium and iron as well as calcium. Tofu thickens and 'smoothes' the taste of blended drinks. Silken tofu does work the best in smoothies – you can add 50-125ml (1-4fl oz) to any of the recipes in this book, or replace the yoghurt or milk where stated. In vegetable smoothies, you can add canned or cooked and puréed soya beans to the recipe to make it even thicker!

!Warning Soya beans and soya products are a common food allergen and some people may be allergic!

!Warning Much of the world's soya bean crop has been genetically modified: if you wish to avoid GM foods, buy organic and certified non-GM soya products!

Coconut milk

You can buy coconut milk in cartons in shops – along with coconut cream – but in general, it has been highly sweetened. The tastiest and most refreshing coconut milk is that straight from the nut – because you'll have worked up a sweat cracking it open! Alternatively, you can make a coconut milk using the shredded flesh – either fresh or dried – of the coconut:

125ml (¼ pint) grated fresh coconut flesh or 75ml (2½fl oz) of dried grated coconut

2-3 drops vanilla essence

125ml (¼ pint) boiling water

Put the coconut into the blender and add the boiling water. Blend on a low speed for around 20 seconds. Gradually (if possible) increase the speed to high and blend for another 20-30 seconds. Allow to cool then refrigerate. It will keep for about a week in the fridge.

Coconut cream

You can buy cans of ready-made coconut cream, but I find that the unsweetened versions taste hideous and the sweetened versions are too sweet! It's actually very easy to make your own:

Take a chilled hard block of pure creamed coconut (usually about 200g/8oz). Grate it to break down the grainy texture. For each rounded tablespoon of grated creamed coconut add a level tablespoon of caster sugar (or slightly less) and mix with a very small amount of hot water to dissolve. Stir until you have a runny, smooth paste. Check for sweetness and allow to cool. Use it the same day otherwise it goes grainy again and rancid!

Fruit and nut milks

Not really milk, but a great way to add a touch of luxury and energy to a smoothie! Fruit milks are made by combining chopped, dried fruits such as apricots or dates with boiling water. They are low in fat and naturally sweet, and they can be used to replace all or some of the liquid in fruit smoothies.

Apricot milk

- *125g (4oz) chopped, dried apricots*
- *2-3 drops vanilla essence*
- *500ml (about 1 pint) boiling water*

Put the dried apricots into the blender with 250ml (½ pint) of boiling water. Put the lid on and blend on a low speed for about 30 seconds. Gradually (if possible) increase the speed to high for a further 30 seconds. With the blender still running, add another 250ml (½ pint) of boiling water and blend for 30 seconds or until smooth. Check the consistency: if necessary, add up to an extra 125ml (¼ pint) of boiling water and blend until smooth. Allow to cool. Covered and refrigerated this will keep for up to one week.

Almond milk

Almonds, as well as cashews and sunflower seeds, can be blanched or soaked and blended with water to produce a delicious and intensely flavoured 'milk' which is high in protein – and in calories. Almonds are rich in minerals, zinc, magnesium, potassium, and iron and also have some B vitamins. They also contain oxalic acid which combines with these minerals to carry them out of your body, so they are best eaten with Vitamin C rich foods for maximum absorption. The less water you use, the thicker the milk, – a rule of thumb is 1 part almonds to 4 parts water. It should be strained before use. Refrigerate the 'milk' and keep it for 2-3 days, stirring well before use.

- *100g (4oz) blanched almonds*
- *1 tbsp honey (optional)*
- *200ml (7fl oz) of water and 3-4 ice cubes*

Put the honey, almond and ice cubes into a blender and blend into a smooth paste. Gradually add the water until the mixture is a smooth, milky consistency. You can add it to smoothies in place of cow's, soya, rice milk, or yoghurt.

Warning! If you have a nut allergy, then you will be allergic to almond milk too!

Yoghurt

One of the most ancient foods, yoghurt, is a superfood: many health problems start in the guts when the balance between the good and bad bacteria is upset. The 'live' or 'bio' yoghurts are the ones that will help restore the balance of the bacteria in the gut, and even people who have trouble digesting milk often find they can cope quite well with yoghurt.

To make your own yoghurt:

- 1 litre (1 ¾ pint) UHT milk (whole) *(I use UHT milk as it only needs warming up to blood heat (not boiling and cooling down) so it's more energy efficient!)*
- 2 tbsp live, natural yoghurt
- 2 tbsp dried milk *(optional, but it makes for a thicker yoghurt)*

Heat the milk gently to blood heat, add the yoghurt and dried milk and mix thoroughly with a plastic spoon (not metal). Pour into a warmed vacuum flask (or into a bowl which can be covered and wrapped in a towel, and left in a warm place like an airing cupboard). Seal the flask and leave overnight. The next day, pour out of the flask into a bowl, stir, cover and chill.

For a thicker, 'Greek Style' yoghurt, pour the yoghurt from the vacuum flask and strain off the whey – the thin liquid – from the thicker yoghurt through a piece of muslin.

When you want to make your next batch of yoghurt, simply use 2 tablespoons of your own home-made yoghurt to 'start' your next batch off.

What to do when your smoothie is too thick or too thin

Since Mother Nature has rarely made any two oranges or two carrots exactly the same, you might find that your smoothie comes out too thick or too thin. It's not a disaster – there are ways of making them smooth!

When fruit smoothies are skinny, add yoghurt, cream or ice cream, or tofu to fruit mixes. If you're feeling virtuous, add a banana instead! A useful thing to remember is that using frozen ingredients – either fruit, vegetables, frozen yoghurt or milk 'ice cubes', ice cream or crushed ice – will make the skinniest smoothies plumper.

When vegetable smoothies are limp, add yoghurt or tofu, cooked rice, barley, or canned and puréed chickpeas or soya beans! You can even put a cooked potato or two in to thicken it up!

When smoothies are too thick, add a little more juice, some ice cubes, mineral water or milk. In vegetable smoothies you could add some vegetable stock, too.

fruit smoothies

Full of flavour and packed with vitamins and minerals, smoothies made from fruit are perhaps the most popular.

Unlike juices, which lack soluble fibre, smoothies deliver all the natural fibre present in the whole fruit. Fruits are high in natural sugars that your body uses as fuel, which makes them a great way to start the day. But smoothies also make a great mid-morning or afternoon 'pick-me up', an energy-booster after work if you're off to the gym or theatre and don't have the time or the inclination to eat first, and a healthy snack for when you just feel peckish. You will find that some blends are so delicious you can serve them to guests as dessert after dinner, or offer them instead of alcoholic beverages or fizzy sodas at parties.

Fruit smoothies are the perfect way to enjoy seasonal fruits: where possible buy organic fruits so that you can reduce the amounts of potentially harmful chemicals used widely in the commercial production of crops. Nevertheless, you are advised always to wash fruit before slicing, and to peel off the skins. If you have a juicer, you can juice many of the fruit skins too, but a blender won't always be effective in chopping skins. Choose ripe fruits. Under-ripe fruits in smoothies won't have the same juiciness and may taste bitter. Don't worry if a fruit is a little soft, it will still make great smoothies, but avoid fruits that are mouldy or rotten, they are starting to ferment and may cause stomach upsets.

Remember, you can use frozen fruits: this makes smoothies that are not only colder, but a little thicker, at least while they are still frozen! If there is a seasonal surfeit of fresh fruit, peel, seed and stone/pit the fruit and cut it into chunks. Arrange the pieces, or individual berries, washed and patted dry, in a single layer on a baking sheet and freeze them until hard. Transfer the fruit to a re-sealable plastic bag, label and seal. The fruit pieces will keep for up to six months in the freezer.

When fresh fruit is not available, canned fruit is a convenient way to make tasty smoothies. Wherever possible, buy organically grown fruit and fruits canned in their own juice, in water or in apple juice. Fruits canned in heavy sugar syrup are OK, but you will be adding extra sugar which you probably don't need! You can drain the syrup from the fruit and rinse in cold water: it won't get rid of all the added sugar, but I'd rather have a slightly sweet smoothy than none at all!

Dried fruit can also be used in smoothies: apricots, apples, raisins, prunes, even berries are available in dried forms, but watch out for commercially dried fruits which have been fumigated with sulphur dioxide, a gas that not only destroys the B vitamins — it is also poisonous! Wherever possible, buy unsulphured fruits and wash thoroughly. If you are hooked on health foods, you can buy domestic food dehydrators and dry your own fruits. This makes great commercial and dietary sense, if you have a ready supply of inexpensive fruit available.

Drying concentrates the sugars and fibres in the fruit so if you use dried fruit, your smoothy will be a little sweeter than one made with fresh fruit and you'll find that the fibre provides more, shall we say, 'cleansing power'! When you use dried fruit in a smoothie recipe, it's a good idea to rehydrate the fruit by covering it with just enough water in a saucepan and heating slowly. When the fruits have become plump, allow them to cool and drain. You can keep the liquid to use in another recipe! Chop the fruit before adding it to the blender.

One last thing: smoothies should be pleasurable, not a form of punishment! Look at the recipes and remember they are suggestions: if you don't like a particular fruit, then don't force yourself to eat or drink it! Have fun with the recipes: increase or decrease the amounts and proportions to suit your tastes.

kiwi-pear

If you're on a bit of a hormone roller coaster try this delightful green juice packed with essential trace minerals to help you stay on the rails.

ingredients

1 kiwi fruit
1 pear, fresh or canned

method

Peel the kiwi and chop it into pieces. Chop the pear, too. Put the fruit into a blender. Blend on a low speed for around 20 seconds. Gradually (if possible) increase the speed to high and blend for another 20-30 seconds.

pink grapefruit, orange & pineapple

Liquid sunshine! Sweet yet sharp, smooth and fresh, this mix is a real winner.

ingredients

1 orange, peeled and broken into segments

1 pink grapefruit, peeled and broken into segments

¼ small pineapple or 2-3 slices of canned fruit in own or apple juice, drained

method

Place the grapefruit, orange and pineapple in the blender. Blend on a low speed for around 20 seconds. Gradually (if possible) increase the speed to high and blend for another 20-30 seconds.

plum punch

This is a delicious 'nectar', packed full of goodness, and especially Vitamins A, E, C and betacarotene. This combination of fruits is guaranteed to lift your spirits and boost your energy levels.

ingredients

1 peach, fresh or canned

1 plum, fresh or canned

1 kiwi fruit

method

Remove the stones, but not the skin, from the peach and the plums and peel the kiwi. Cut the fruit into chunks, reserving a slice or two of plum for garnish. Blend on a low speed for around 20 seconds. Gradually (if possible) increase the speed to high and blend for another 20-30 seconds.

holiday

Bromelain in pineapple is a 'fat buster', and mango will provide you with your daily requirement of Vitamin C, two-thirds of your vitamin A, half of your vitamin E and almost a quarter of your fibre. These fruits are wonderful foods for slimmers, as their natural sweetness means you won't want to snack on junk food.

ingredients

1 small banana
½ mango
¼ pineapple (or 3 slices of canned fruit in own juice, drained)
tonic water or sparkling mineral water (optional)

method

Peel the banana, mango and pineapple. Blend on a low speed for around 20 seconds. Gradually (if possible) increase the speed to high and blend for another 20-30 seconds. If the mix is a little too thick, dilute with tonic or sparkling mineral water. Pour into a glass over ice cubes if you wish. You can make a longer drink by topping with mineral or tonic water.

after eight

This can be 8am or 8pm! Over ice, it's lovely on a balmy summer evening. You can use a good dash of ready-made, organic, pressed apple juice instead of the juiced apple.

ingredients

2 kiwi fruits

1 apple, or a small glass of apple juice

8 springs of mint, 1 set aside for garnish

method

Wash, core and chop the apple and peel the kiwis and chop into chunks. Chop the mint. Put the fruit and mint into the blender. Blend on a low speed for around 20 seconds. Gradually (if possible) increase the speed to high and blend for another 20-30 seconds. (If you are using ready-made apple juice, add this to the blended kiwis and mint mix.) Pour into a glass and decorate with a sprig of mint.

papaya power

With vitamin A, C and carotenoids, papaya is antibacterial, antioxidant and detoxifying and can help prevent skin disorders.

ingredients

1 papaya, peeled and de-stoned
juice of 1 lemon, or whole lemon peeled

method

Pop the fruit into a blender/food processor and blend together until smooth. Pour into a glass and garnish with a slice of lemon.

pink pineapple

Pineapples are not fruits in the ordinary sense of the word: they are, in fact, multiple organs that form when the fruits of around one hundred flowers coalesce!

ingredients

¼ pineapple (or 3 thick slices of canned fruit in its own juice, drained)

1 orange, a blood orange will add an even deeper colour

150g (5oz) strawberries

method

Peel the pineapple and the orange. Wash the strawberries and remove the stalks. Place the fruit into a blender and blend together until smooth. Garnish with a strawberry – if there are any left!

four fruit energy

This is a terrific spring tonic, excellent for dispelling those winter blues and getting the sap rising!

ingredients

½ papaya

1 kiwi fruit

1 orange

½ grapefruit, a pink one if possible!

method

Peel the papaya and scoop out the seeds. Peel the kiwi and keep a slice for decoration. In a blender/food processor, blend the papaya and kiwi together into a purée. Peel and juice the grapefruit and orange, or just peel and drop the fruits into the blender and combine the juices with the fruit purée. Blend on a low speed for around 20 seconds. Gradually (if possible) increase the speed to high and blend for another 20-30 seconds. If a little too thick, add a splash of mineral water. Pour into a glass and decorate with slices of kiwi and orange.

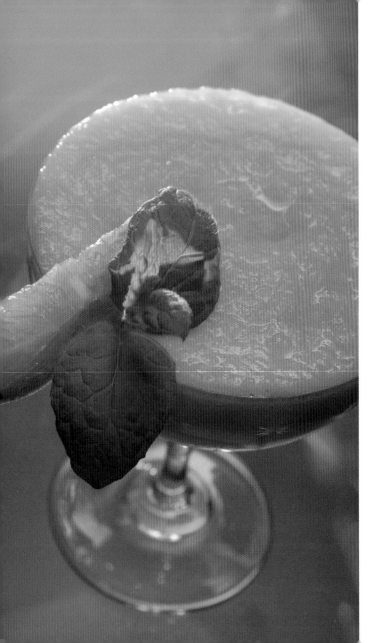

orange pear

A very simple and delicious drink, guaranteed to help you unwind and de-stress at the end of a long day. Pears are a good source of pectin – a great bowel regulator – and they sweep cholesterol from the body.

ingredients

3 oranges

1 pear

method

Peel the oranges and remove the stalk from the pear. Cut into chunks and place the fruit in a blender/food processor. Blend on a low speed for around 20 seconds. Gradually (if possible) increase the speed to high and blend for another 20-30 seconds. Pour into a glass and garnish with a slice of orange.

pear, lemon & mint

Rich in soluble fibre, pears are infinitely more attractive than bran! The delicate flavour is here enhanced by the sharp lemon and fresh mint.

ingredients

2-3 pears, fresh or canned

juice of ½ lemon

6-8 mint leaves, chopped

method

Core and cut the pears into chunks if using fresh. Chop the mint and squeeze the lemon. Place the pears, mint and lemon juice in the blender and blend on a low speed for around 20 seconds. Gradually (if possible) increase the speed to high and blend for another 20-30 seconds.

raspberry nectar

Rich in Vitamin B, this lovely drink will 'de-frazzle' nerves and give a well-deserved boost to both body and spirit, especially when you smell the lovely scents of fruit and lemon balm or mint.

ingredients

80g (3oz) raspberries, fresh, frozen or canned

1 peach, fresh or canned

sprig of mint

method

Rinse the raspberries and pat dry. De-stone the peach and cut into quarters. Place the fruit in a blender. Blend on a low speed for around 20 seconds. Gradually (if possible) increase the speed to high and blend for another 20-30 seconds. Pour into a glass and decorate with a sprig of mint.

mango fix

This is guaranteed to satisfy the craving for something sweet and give you a real lift, but without the low experienced immediately after snacking on something like chocolate! Just the flowery aroma of juiced mango and pineapple is enough to get you up and at it!

ingredients

1 mango
½ pineapple, or 4-6 slices canned fruit

method

Cut the pineapple from the skin if using fresh, and wash, peel and de-stone the mango. Blend on a low speed for around 20 seconds. Gradually (if possible) increase the speed to high and blend for another 20-30 seconds.

apple pie

This is a really delicious morning mix: apples are an excellent source of pectin and fibre, with cinnamon, nutmeg* and ginger. You can even add a spoonful of rolled oats! Or in the evening, why not add a splash of Calvados or Applejack – for purely medicinal reasons, of course!

ingredients

60ml (2fl oz) apple juice

1 small apple, cored and chopped

1 small bunch of red grapes (or a small glass of red grape juice)

1 wedge of lemon, peeled and chopped

pinch ground cinnamon

pinch ground nutmeg*

pinch ground ginger

method

Place the fruit and the juices into the blender. Blend on a low speed for around 20 seconds. Gradually (if possible) increase the speed to high and blend for another 20-30 seconds.

*Because of its strong volatile oils, nutmeg is best avoided if you are pregnant.

watermelon splash

Melons belong to the same family of plants as cucumbers, pumpkins, marrows and gourds and have been cultivated in Asia since ancient times. They were introduced into Europe in the late 16th century. Cooling and refreshing, watermelons contain vitamins A and C, iron and potassium.

ingredients

1 orange, peeled and broken into segments
1 tsp lemon juice
1 slice of watermelon, about 1cm (½in) thick, peeled and de-seeded
1 plum, fresh or canned, peeled and chopped

method

Place the fruit into the blender. Blend on a low speed for around 20 seconds. Gradually (if possible) increase the speed to high and blend for another 20-30 seconds.

You can replace the plum with a nectarine or a few strawberries if you like. And try lime juice instead of lemon for a tasty zing!

think pink

A perfect colour for summer, and it,s good for you too!
Watermelons are thought to be antibacterial and anticancer.
They are also gently stimulating on the kidneys.

ingredients

1 tsp lemon or lime juice

1 slice of watermelon, about 2.5cm (1in) thick, peeled and
  de-seeded

8 pitted cherries, fresh or canned

8 raspberries, fresh, frozen or canned

1 good splash of cranberry juice

method

Put the watermelon, cherries and raspberries into the blender
with the lemon/lime juice and blend together on a low speed
for about 20 seconds. Stop the machine and pour in the splash
of cranberry juice, just enough to thin the mix. Blend on a high
speed for another 20-30 seconds.

magic mango

The mango is a power-house of goodness: one of these fruits provides a complete day's vitamin C, two-thirds of your vitamin A, nearly half of your Vitamin E, and a quarter of your fibre needs. Make sure this magic fruit becomes part of your weekly shopping list!

ingredients

1 mango, peeled, pitted and chopped

1 slice watermelon, about 2.5cm (1in) thick, peeled and de-seeded

1 small bunch of red grapes, or a splash of red grape juice

method

Put the mango, watermelon and grapes into the blender. If you use grape juice, wait until the two fruits are blended to add just enough to thicken the mix a little. Blend on a low speed for around 20 seconds. Gradually (if possible) increase the speed to high and blend for another 20-30 seconds.

typically tropical

Here's how to make sure you get your recommended five portions of fruit/vegetables in a delicious mix! Packed with Vitamin C and betacarotene which is then converted by the body into Vitamin A, this mix is a great 'skin protector'.

ingredients

1 orange, peeled and broken into segments

½ mango, peeled, pitted and chopped

1 slice pineapple, fresh or canned

1 slice watermelon, about 2.5cm (1in) thick, peeled, de-seeded and chopped

1 slice of papaya (paw paw) about 2.5cm (1in) thick, fresh or canned

5 strawberries, fresh, frozen or canned

method

Place all the fruit in the blender and blend on a low speed for around 20 seconds. Then increase the speed to high and blend for another 20-30 seconds.

kiwi-lime

Kiwi fruits are terrific for boosting the immune system,
and they contain twice as much Vitamin C as an orange
and more fibre than an apple! Papayas, with their yellow
flesh, are a source of betacarotene, and one fruit
provides about a quarter of your daily Vitamin A needs.

ingredients

125ml (3½fl oz) white grape juice
2 tbsp lime juice
2 kiwi fruits, peeled and chopped
½ papaya, de-seeded if preferred, chopped

method

Place the kiwis and papaya into the blender along with the
white grape juice and lime juice. Blend on a low speed for
around 20 seconds, then gradually increase the speed to high
and blend for another 20-30 seconds.

raspberry, apple & rosewater smoothie

Rosewater is used extensively in the Middle East in food and drinks and is made from steeping rose petals in alcohol. Apples will slowly release their sugar, while raspberries are packed with Vitamin C.

ingredients

1 apple, cored and chopped

1 tsp honey (optional)

1 tbsp lemon juice

125g (4oz) fresh or frozen raspberries

125ml (3½fl oz) apple juice

1-2 tbsp rosewater

method

Put the chopped apple into the blender with the honey and lemon juice and blend well until smooth, pushing the mixture down the sides of the jug/bowl if necessary. Add the raspberries and blend until smooth. Pour in the rosewater and blend briefly to combine.

marvellous melon

Melon and ginger is a classic combination, and cantaloupe melons are especially valued for their diuretic, low-sodium and antioxidant properties. While the melon cools, the ginger stimulates the blood circulation and helps rid the body of toxins. Pears are an excellent source of soluble pectin, a useful bowel regulator. These clever fruits don't just lower cholesterol, they actually eliminate it from the body!

ingredients

¼ cantaloupe melon, peeled and de-seeded
1 pear, cored and chopped, fresh or canned
1cm (½in) fresh ginger, finely chopped
sprig of mint

method

Place the chopped fruit and the ginger into the blender and blend on a low speed until combined. Then briefly blend on a high speed for about 20 seconds.

waterfall

Grapes, pears and melons are delicious when combined and they have the added bonus of 'strengthening' the kidneys. If you can't get your hands on grapes, use a couple of apples instead.

ingredients

125g (4oz) green or yellow grapes, cut into halves
2 pears, cored and chopped, fresh or canned
¼ cantaloupe melon, peeled, de-seeded and chopped
pinch of ground ginger

method

Wash and dry the grapes and cut them into half. Put the grapes, the pear flesh and the chopped melon into the blender. Blend on a low speed for around 20 seconds. Gradually (if possible) increase the speed to high and blend for another 20-30 seconds. If the mixture is a little too thick for your taste, add a splash of apple or white grape juice. Dust with a pinch of ground ginger.

big breakfast

Start the day with this power-packed smoothie. The carbohydrate in bananas are 'slow release', so you'll feel sustained for longer and won't get a sudden high followed by an equally sudden low. Mixed with orange, your taste buds will be woken up too!

ingredients

¼ mango, fresh or canned, chopped

1 small banana

1 orange, peeled and broken into segments

1 tbsp wheat bran

½ tbsp sesame seeds

1 tsp honey (optional)

method

Put the mango, banana and orange into the blender with the honey (optional). Blend until smooth on a low speed. Add the wheat bran and sesame seeds and blend again on a high speed until smooth and creamy.

kiwi & stem ginger

Use lovely plump, ripe kiwis for the sweetest and most intense flavour. If yours are a little under-ripe, put them into a sealed plastic bag with an apple, a pear or a banana and they will soon be perfect for eating! This recipe uses preserved stem ginger and a little of the syrup from the jar.

ingredients

2 kiwi fruits, peeled and chopped
1 piece preserved stem ginger, chopped
1 tbsp syrup from the ginger jar
chilled sparkling mineral water (optional)

method

Put the kiwis, the ginger syrup and the chopped stem ginger into the blender and blend on a low speed until smooth, then blend again on a high speed for 15-20 seconds. Pour into a glass and, if you like, top with sparkling mineral water.

orange & passion fruit medley

Passion fruits have a sweet, golden flesh and numerous black, edible seeds that get stuck in your teeth! The best way to enjoy a passion fruit is in a smoothie, and the seeds look gorgeous suspended in the mix. An additional flavour and fragrance is brought to this smoothie by cardamom.

ingredients

½ tbsp ground dried cardamom seeds

1 tsp honey

1 passion fruit

2 oranges peeled and broken into segments (or 125ml/ 3½fl oz orange juice)

method

Crush the cardamon seeds in a mortar with a pestle. Cut the passion fruit in half and scoop out the flesh and seeds. Put the cardamom, passion fruit and oranges/orange juice into the blender with the honey and blend on low speed until smooth, then blend for 15-20 seconds on high speed.

plum passion

The combination of plum and passion fruit is surprisingly nice, and the banana makes for extra creaminess! If you don't want the passion fruit seeds in your drink, then strain the flesh through a sieve first.

ingredients

1 passion fruit

1 plum, de-stoned and chopped, you can use fresh or canned

1 small banana

1-2 tsp lemon juice, according to taste.

method

Cut the passion fruit in half and scoop out the flesh and seeds (strain through a sieve if you don't want the seeds). Put the flesh into the blender and add the chopped plum, the banana and the lemon juice. Blend on a low speed for around 20 seconds. Gradually (if possible) increase the speed to high and blend for another 20-30 seconds.

gooseberry fool

Gooseberries, so named because they were traditionally served with roasted goose, have the sharpest taste, but here, combined with sweet apples and kiwis, their tartness is mellowed into a delightful, fresh-tasting drink.

ingredients

1 kiwi fruit, peeled and chopped

100g (about 3oz) gooseberries, fresh or canned in own juice

1 apple, or a small glass of apple juice

1 pear, cored and chopped, fresh or canned

method

Put the chopped fruit into the blender. Blend on a low speed for around 20 seconds. Gradually (if possible) increase the speed to high and blend for another 20-30 seconds.

cherry berry

This is one of those mixes that, in spite of its health-giving benefits, never ceases to make one feel a little bit guilty, it's just so delicious and it's hard to believe that there's no added sugar!

ingredients

75g (2½oz) red cherries, pitted, or you can use canned fruit
100g (about 3oz) red grapes, cut in half
110g (about 3oz) strawberries, fresh, frozen or canned

method

Stone the cherries, cut the grapes and strawberries in half and place them all in the blender and blend on a low speed until smooth. Blend briefly at high speed for about 15 seconds.

soothing smoothie

You can't get a smoothie simpler than this, and it's wonderful on dry or sore throats. In the depths of winter you can if you want use canned or frozen fruit, but use fruits canned in their own or in apple juice to avoid unnecessary sugar.

ingredients

1 peach or nectarine, stoned and chopped
200g (7oz) strawberries, hulled and halved

method

Put the peach or nectarine into the blender with the strawberries. Blend on a low speed for around 20 seconds. Gradually (if possible) increase the speed to high and blend for another 20-30 seconds.

apricot & lime

Fresh apricots appear and then disappear! Their name is derived from the Latin *praecoquum* meaning 'early ripe', and the English called them 'hastie peche' because they were among the first fresh fruits to appear in summer. Buy as many as you can while they are around! If not, use canned fruits or even dried fruits that have been rehydrated.

ingredients

juice of 1 lime

2 oranges, peeled and broken into segments,

4 apricots, fresh, canned or dried and rehydrated by covering with just enough water in a saucepan and heating slowly. When plump, allow to cool and drain.

2-3 sprigs of lemon balm, chopped finely

method

Place the fruit into the blender with the chopped lemon balm and lime juice and blend on a low speed for around 20 seconds. Gradually (if possible) increase the speed to high and blend for another 20-30 seconds. Pour into a glass and decorate with a sprig of lemon balm.

tropical fruit cyclone

100% pure fruit, nothing added or taken away. It'll blow away the cobwebs, shake up your taste buds, make your eyes shine, your hair bright and your skin glow. Why it's almost like being in love! You can use fresh or canned fruit, just make sure it's in its own juice, or in apple juice, not in heavy sugar syrup!

ingredients

¼ pineapple, peeled and chopped, or 4 thick slices of canned fruit, drained

1 small mango, fresh or canned (in own or apple juice and drained)

½ small papaya, fresh or canned (in own or apple juice and drained)

method

Place the fruit in the blender and blend until smooth on a low speed. Turn up the speed to high for about another 15 seconds.

grapefruit & pear

Grapefruit is one of those fruits people either love or hate! If you're inclined to avoid it, then go for the pink version instead! The pink colour is natural, and these ruby red glories were only discovered growing in the Rio Grande Valley of Texas in 1929. Isn't Nature kind!

ingredients

1 pink grapefruit, peeled and broken into segments
1 pear, cored and chopped

method

Put the grapefruit and pear into the blender and blend on a low speed until smooth.

clementine, strawberry & banana smoothie

A gorgeous pink colour and thick and creamy, but no dairy produce in sight. You can use clementines, tangerines, mandarins or satsumas – or why not try a tangelo, a cross between a tangerine and a grapefruit.

ingredients

1 banana

3 clementines or mandarins, tangerines or satsumas, fresh or canned in their own juice, drained

6 strawberries, fresh frozen or canned and drained

2 ice cubes

method

Peel the banana and citrus fruits if using fresh. Hull the strawberries. Put all the fruit into the blender. Blend on a low speed for around 20 seconds. Gradually (if possible) increase the speed to high and blend for another 20-30 seconds.

tangerine & mango smoothie

Mango flesh makes perfect, thick luscious smoothies which are high in betacarotene, giving the body its vital Vitamin A. There are over one thousand varieties of mango known, ranging in size and shape from round and avocado-shaped to long and narrow, and from the size of an egg, to well over 2.5kg (5lb). This wonderful tropical fruit is in fact a relative of the cashew!

ingredients

3 tangerines, fresh or canned in own juice and drained
½ small mango, fresh or canned

method

Peel the mango and tangerines if using fresh. Put the fruits into the blender and blend slowly for about 20 seconds on a low speed, then increase the speed to high and blend for 15-20 seconds more.

mandarin &
papaya smoothie

This lovely thick and smooth mix has a delicate taste. Papayas (or paw paws) are low in calories but high in Vitamin A. If you are using fresh papaya, you'll find the centre of the fruit is packed with edible but bitter peppercorn-like seeds.

ingredients

½ small papaya, fresh or canned

1 small banana

3 mandarins (or other small citrus fruit, fresh or canned in own juice and drained)

method

Cut the papaya in half if using fresh, and scoop out the seeds and discard. Scoop out the flesh and place in the blender. Peel the banana and break into pieces and add to the blender. Peel the mandarins and break into segments. Add these to the blender. Blend on a low speed for around 20 seconds. Gradually (if possible) increase the speed to high and blend for another 20-30 seconds.

mango, raspberry & lime smoothie

This is an inspired combination: the flavours of each fruit are really clear on the palate and you are providing yourself with loads of Vitamin C, betacarotene and fibre.

ingredients

¼ mango (fresh or canned)
10 raspberries – fresh, frozen or canned
juice of 1 lime
mineral water (optional)

method

Put the mango and raspberries into the blender with the juice of the lime and blend until smooth. If you want your smoothie a little less thick, blend with a little mineral water, adding a dash at a time on a slow speed.

pineapple, melon & mint

The cleansing properties of melon combined with the vitamins and minerals of pineapple are a real body booster. The fragrance of the mint will lift your spirits, warm you up a little, then cool and refresh you.

ingredients

¼ small honeydew melon, seeds removed
¼ small pineapple, or 3 thick slices of canned fruit, cut into chunks
small bunch of mint

method

Chop the mint, melon and pineapple, catching every drop of juice over the blender jug! Blend on a low speed for around 20 seconds. Gradually (if possible) increase the speed to high and blend for another 20-30 seconds.

grape & papaya

Grapes contain a huge number of aromatic compounds – more than any other fruit! The most important of these are astringent tannins, flavones, anthocyanine, linalo, gernaniol and nerol, all contributing to the anticancer properties of the grape. Nourishing, strengthening and cleansing, don't wait until you get ill to eat them! Combined with the Vitamin C in papaya to boost the body's immune system, betacarotene to keep your skin in tip-top condition and fibre to help reduce cholesterol, this mix is made in heaven!

ingredients

½ papaya, de-seeded (or canned, in own or apple juice)
small bunch of green grapes, about 15 fruits in all, cut in half
mineral water (optional)

method

Put the papaya and grapes into the blender and blend until smooth. You can make the mixture a little less thick by adding mineral water a splash at a time and blending again.

passion fruit, lime & orange

Packed full of vitamin C this is a refreshingly smooth yet sharp-tasting mix. The colour is even better if you use blood oranges!

ingredients

2 oranges, peeled and broken into segments
2 passion fruits
juice of 1 lime

method

Peel and break the oranges into segments. Cut the passion fruits in half and scoop out the flesh. Place the fruit into a blender with the juice of a lime and blend on a low speed for around 20 seconds. Gradually (if possible) increase the speed to high and blend for another 20-30 seconds.

peach &
strawberry

A thick golden drink flecked with pink, you could add a splash of chilled sparkling white wine or champagne for a summer party!

ingredients

1 peach, stoned (pitted) (or use canned in own or apple juice)

1 small orange, peeled and broken into segments

6 strawberries, hulled and cut in half – fresh, frozen or canned – or raspberries if you prefer

mineral water (optional)

method

Slice the peach into the blender, add the orange segments and the strawberries. Blend until smooth, adding a dash of mineral water if too thick.

raspberry & blood orange

Raspberries are highly prized for their cooling effects, ideal if you are feeling feverish. They are also astringent and therefore terrific for the digestive tract and are helpful in healing sore gums. With added Vitamin C from the blood oranges, this will help to revive you if you are feeling under the weather.

ingredients

2 blood oranges
125g (4oz) raspberries, fresh, frozen or canned
mineral water (optional)

method

Peel the oranges and break into segments. Place the oranges and the raspberries into the blender and blend until smooth. If a little too thick, add a little mineral water, a splash at a time, and blend again.

cranberry crush

For centuries North American Indians used cranberries for both food and medicine. The hippuric acid in cranberry juice is antibacterial and is known to be beneficial in treating both acute and chronic cystitis.

ingredients

125g (4oz) cranberries, fresh, frozen or dried and rehydrated by covering with just enough water in a saucepan and heating slowly. When plump, allow to cool and drain.

2 oranges, peeled and broken into segments

1 lemon, squeezed, or peeled and added whole to the blender

method

Put the cranberries, oranges and lemon/lemon juice into the blender. Blend on a low speed for around 20 seconds. Gradually (if possible) increase the speed to high and blend for another 20-30 seconds.

very berry best

This mix combines some of the tastiest fruits, fruits which we all too often think of as an indulgence. The total cost is probably no more than a cup of take-away coffee and it's so much better for your health. You can vary the quantities and types of berries as you like. Just choose your favourites!

ingredients

75g (about 2oz or so) raspberries – fresh, frozen or canned
75g (about 2oz or so) blueberries – fresh, frozen or canned
75g (about 2oz or so) pitted cherries – fresh, canned or bottled
75g (about 2oz or so) grapes, cut in half
1 pear, or a slice of melon, peeled and chopped

method

Put the berries, cherries and grapes into the blender. Add the chopped pear or melon. Blend on a low speed for around 20 seconds. Gradually (if possible) increase the speed to high and blend for another 20-30 seconds.

raspberry, orange & pear zinger

Packed full of Vitamin C, this is guaranteed to tickle your taste buds – and help firm up those gums! The natural sugar and soluble fibre in the pears will also help to boost your energy and keep your intestines in tip-top working order!

ingredients

2 oranges, peeled and broken into segments
150 g (about 5oz) raspberries – fresh, frozen, canned or bottled
1 ripe pear, peeled and cored, fresh or canned

method

Put the oranges, the pear and the raspberries into the blender and blend on a low speed until smooth. Increse the speed to high and blend for another 20 seconds or so.

morning
good mood

Start the day as you mean to go on, feeling good and looking great! In fact, if you can replace all your teas, coffees, sodas (and booze!) for two or three days with glasses of this beauty instead, you'll notice the difference in your lighter mood, your energy levels and your appearance. Give it a try!

ingredients

100ml (3½ fl oz) white or red/purple grape juice
  (or you can throw in a good handful of grapes!)
2 oranges, peeled and broken into segments
1 pear, cored and chopped, or canned in its own or
  apple juice, drained

method

Put the grapes/grape juice, the oranges and the pear in the blender. Blend on a low speed for 20 seconds. Gradually increase the speed to high and blend for another 20-30 seconds.

mellow melon

A very easy blend that will restore lost energy. With vitamins and minerals in abundance, this drink beats any canned confection any day! Cantaloupe melons help to increase the release of energy from other foods and have high levels of carotenoids which may inhibit the formation of cancerous cells.

ingredients

½ cantaloupe melon, de-seeded, and cut into chunks
2 oranges, peeled and broken into segments

method

Put the melon and the oranges into the blender and blend until smooth.

vegetable smoothies

Eat your greens and reds, oranges and yellows! The terrific thing about vegetable smoothies is that they are one tasty way to make sure you get enough fresh vegetables to keep you in good health.

Like fruits, vegetable smoothies boost your energy levels, are packed with beneficial vitamins and minerals and are quick to make. You have the added bonus of being able to enjoy them cold or, if you like, heat them up into a nutritious and warming soup.

As with fruit, whenever possible select organic vegetables and store them correctly: they will stay fresher in the crisper drawer of your fridge.

Unlike using a juicing machine, which will extract the juice out of any vegetable and leave behind the fibre, using a blender gives you all the goodness of the vegetable. The problem is, of course, that some vegetables are hard when raw. So, in a blender, you will get a purée of the vegetable which can be mixed with a commercially made juice such as tomato, carrot or apple, or yoghurt, milk (including soya, rice, goat and ewe's milk) or tofu.

One way to overcome the hardness of vegetables is to cook them first! Chop and steam or parboil carrots, potatoes, leeks and celery, or put the raw vegetables into the blender, purée them and cook them like a soup. Cooking vegetables first not only softens the texture but the flavour, too, which can be useful with strong-tasting ingredients such as onions. Roasting vegetables before using them in smoothies gives a rich, sweet taste. Don't forget to save any cooked, leftover veggies for use in smoothies!

There is an increasing number of ready-prepared vegetable juices available, but in most instances, these won't have the fibre that is vital to our well-being. Nevertheless, because smoothies need to have a somewhat liquid base, by all means use ready-made canned or cartonned juices.

You can also happily use canned and frozen vegetables. They save cooking time and, in most instances, won't have lost any of the nutritional value in the process. Once again, the range of organic produce in both canned and frozen varieties is increasing. Unsalted, water-packed organic vegetables and fresh vegetables can be used interchangeably in the recipes.

Don't forget that you can make a smoothie thicker by adding yoghurt, tofu, puréed, cooked soya beans, a handful of rolled oats, or some barley flakes. A cooked potato added to the mix will also bulk it out. Fruit and nut milks (see pages 30-1 for recipes) give an extra texture, flavour and a little sweetness to vegetable smoothies. If you need to extend a recipe to make a smoothy into a skinnier soup, you can always add some consommé, vegetable stock or miso.

Get adventurous and let your taste buds guide you to new sensations. The recipes are suggestions: if you like your smoothies thicker or thinner, hot or cold, spicy or neutral, make them that way. If you don't like a particular vegetable, don't use it! After all, a 'little of what you fancy does you good', so make smoothies a pleasure!

pine-carrot

Carrots are exceptionally versatile vegetables that are naturally sweet. They can be added to any smoothie recipe and they can be used raw. But cooking (try parboiling them) frees up those valuable carotenes, the precursors to Vitamin A, the anticancer agents. They also help prevent the appearance of wrinkles! Pineapple is full of fibre and is used in folk medicine to help relieve hot, sore throats.

ingredients

2 large carrots, cooked and chopped, or 1 can of carrots, or
   100ml/3½fl oz carrot juice
1 wedge pineapple, chopped, or 3-4 slices canned fruit in own
   or apple juice
1 small banana, peeled and chopped
5-6 mint leaves, chopped

method

Put the carrots or carrot juice into the blender with the pineapple, banana and chopped mint. Blend on a low speed for around 20 seconds. Gradually (if possible) increase the speed to high and blend for another 20-30 seconds.

fennel fuel

In ancient Greece, Olympic athletes were fed fennel to boost their strength and fitness. With its distinct anise taste, fennel is a good source of Vitamin A. Cabbage, in all its shapes, forms and colours, is high in cancer-fighting indoles and a good source of choline, vital for mental function. So, this mix feeds both body and mind!

ingredients

½ small red cabbage, raw or steamed to soften it, chopped
½ Florence fennel bulb, chopped, raw or steamed to soften it
2 apples, cored and chopped
1 tbsp lemon juice

method

Place the cabbage and the fennel in the blender with the lemon juice and apples. Blend on a low speed for around 20 seconds. Gradually, (if possible) increase the speed to high and blend for another 20-30 seconds.

beetroot, carrot & orange

Beetroots are full of Vitamin A and the enzyme betaine which nourishes and strengthens the liver and gallbladder. The ancient Greeks so revered this root that it was offered on a silver platter as a tribute to the god Apollo in the temple at Delphi. Mere mortals will benefit from this too!

ingredients

1 large carrot, cooked, or small can of cooked carrots or 85ml (about 3fl oz) carrot juice

½ small beetroot, cooked and chopped

1 blood orange, peeled and broken into segments

method

Place the cooked carrot or carrot juice into the blender with the chopped beetroot and the blood orange. Blend on a low speed for around 20 seconds. Gradually (if possible) increase the speed to high and blend for another 20-30 seconds.

pleasing peas

Peas are an excellent source of dietary fibre and thiamine (Vitamin B1). Unfortunately, peas also contain quite substantial amounts of phytate, which can reduce the bio-availability of minerals such as iron, zinc and calcium. While peas are probably the most widely eaten vegetable, don't make them the only one you eat!

ingredients

1 can peas, about 398ml (14oz), or try sliced green beans

2 carrots, cooked and chopped or 1 can carrots

small piece of fresh fennel chopped, about one-sixth of a bulb is about right

1 apple, cored and chopped

method

Put the peas, carrots, chopped fennel and chopped apple into the blender. Blend on a low speed for around 20 seconds. Gradually (if possible) increase the speed to high and blend for another 20-30 seconds.

potassium power punch

Potassium is vital to every cell in the body, but its enemy is sodium (salt) which means that, with our Western diet, we are often lacking in this vital ingredient. Spinach is rich in potassium as well as calcium, protein, iron, folic acid – a heart protector – and choline, which improves mental ability and concentration and is high in Vitamin E.

ingredients

125g (4oz) blackcurrants, blueberries or blackberries, fresh, frozen, canned or bottled

6-8 spinach leaves chopped, fresh or frozen spinach is fine

2 oranges, peeled and broken into segments, or 100ml (3½fl oz) of orange juice

method

Combine the spinach, berries and oranges in the blender. Blend on a low speed for around 20 seconds. Gradually (if possible) increase the speed to high and blend for another 20-30 seconds.

vegetable smoothies **85**

beetroot, celery & apple

If you've really been struggling with tiredness, with ME or TATT (Tired All The Time Syndrome), recovering from glandular fever or recovering from any other illness or injury, then you need this! Beetroot increases the cellular uptake of oxygen by as much as 400%!

ingredients

1 small cooked beetroot
1 small apple, cored and chopped or 85ml (about 3fl oz) of apple juice
1 large stalk of celery, chopped

method

Put the cooked beetroot, apple (or apple juice) and chopped celery into the blender. Blend on a low speed for around 20 seconds. Gradually (if possible) increase the speed to high and blend for another 20-30 seconds.

carrot & mango

There are 8,000 IU of betacarotene in one single mango, two-thirds of your daily Vitamin A needs. These tropical delights, which have been eaten for over 4,000 years in their native India, will also give you more than a day's supply of Vitamin C, half your Vitamin E and a quarter of your fibre needs, as well as potassium and iron. With carrots and oranges in the mix, you've got a skin tonic, eye brightener and anticancer 'medicine' in a glass, and it tastes terrific too!

ingredients

1 orange, peeled and broken into segments
½ mango, peeled and stoned, or used canned fruit
4 medium cooked carrots, or a can of cooked carrots

method

Put the mango, the orange and the carrots into the blender. Blend on a low speed for around 20 seconds. Gradually (if possible) increase the speed to high and blend for another 20-30 seconds.

well woman

Celery is a rich source of folate, an excellent source for women planning to become pregnant, as well as Vitamin C, potassium and fibre. Grapes are antioxidant, anti-viral, strengthening, cleansing and regenerative, which is why sick people in hospital are given gifts of grapes! They also contain boron, which helps maintain oestrogen levels, thus preventing calcium loss and osteoporosis.

ingredients

2 large celery stalks

large bunch, about 30 green grapes, halved

method

Put the celery and the grapes into the blender. Blend on a low speed for around 20 seconds. Gradually (if possible) increase the speed to high and blend for another 20-30 seconds.

celery, tomato & apple

Celery contains magnesium, which is calming for shattered nerves. This is enhanced by the glutamic acid in tomatoes which is converted in the body to gama-aminobutyric acid (GABA), a calming agent which is known to be effective in reducing kidney hypertension. The apples add just a touch of sweetness to this perfect drink for the end of a stressful day.

ingredients

2 large stalks of celery, chopped

100ml (3½fl oz) tomato juice

1 small tomato, peeled, de-seeded and chopped

1 apple, cored and chopped

method

Put the chopped celery, the tomato, the apple and the tomato juice into the blender. Blend on a low speed for around 20 seconds. Gradually (if possible) increase the speed to high and blend for another 20-30 seconds.

ginger-beet

Ginger is a cleansing and warming herb, stimulating the blood flow to the digestive system and increasing the absorption of nutrients. It is also believed to protect the liver against toxins and help prevent the formation of ulcers. Also excellent for the liver is beetroot. It's the enzyme betaine which strengthens and nourishes.

ingredients

60ml (2fl oz) apple juice

½ stalk celery, chopped

1 small apple, cored and chopped

2-3 small cooked beetroot, chopped

1cm (½ in) chopped chilli pepper

½ clove garlic, chopped

1 piece (1cm/½in) fresh ginger, peeled and chopped

method

Combine the cooked beets with chopped apple, apple juice and chopped celery in the blender with the ginger, chilli and garlic. Blend on a low speed for around 20 seconds. Gradually (if possible) increase the speed to high and blend for another 20-30 seconds.

apple, beet & pear

Possibly one of the oldest cultivated fruits, pears are excellent colon protectors, packed with Vitamin C, boron and potassium, they are also a tasty source of fibre. Apples, even just the smell of apples, help reduce blood pressure!

ingredients

75g (about 2oz) cooked diced beetroot
2 tsp lemon juice
60ml (3½fl oz) apple juice
1 pear, cored and chopped
1 apple, cored and chopped
5-6 fresh spinach leaves, chopped

method

Put the cooked beets into the blender with the apple juice and lemon juice. Add the chopped pear and apple and the chopped spinach leaves. Blend on a low speed for around 20 seconds. Gradually (if possible) increase the speed to high and blend for another 20-30 seconds.

liquid lunch

This is a real 'meal in a glass': it's terrific if you are watching your weight because you will get energy, vitamins, minerals and fibre without the empty calories of highly processed food or snacks. If you want a little more sweetness, add an orange or apple to the mix.

ingredients

2 carrots, cooked and chopped, or a can of cooked carrots

½ cucumber, peeled, de-seeded and chopped

2 stalks celery, chopped

½ small beetroot, cooked and chopped

1 small orange or apple (optional)

method

Put the carrots, cucumber, celery and beetroot into the blender (along with the apple/orange if using) and blend on a low speed for around 20 seconds. Gradually (if possible) increase the speed to high and blend for another 20-30 seconds. Sprinkle with fresh, chopped thyme.

carrot zinger

Carrots originated in Afghanistan and are derived from the wild carrot known as Queen Anne's Lace. They are naturally sweet so adding a little ginger (which for centuries has been used to ease nausea) spices up the flavour.

ingredients

4 carrots, cooked and chopped or one large can of carrots, or 150ml (4½fl oz) carrot juice
1 piece fresh ginger, about 1cm (½in), peeled and chopped

method

Put the orange and the cooked carrots in the blender with the chopped ginger. Blend on a low speed for around 20 seconds. Gradually (if possible) increase the speed to high and blend for another 20-30 seconds.

spiked tomato

Tomato juice is a firm favourite and provides the basis of the famous vodka-based drink, the Bloody Mary. Try this 'Virgin Mary' as an aperitif!

ingredients

3 small tomatoes, peeled and chopped

2 tsp lemon juice

3 tsp Worcester sauce

1 tsp soy sauce

¼ red chilli, de-seed and finely chopped

½ red pepper, chopped

pinch cayenne pepper

pinch of dried thyme, or small bunch fresh, chopped finely

method

Place all the ingredients into the blender and blend on a low speed for around 20 seconds. Gradually (if possible) increase the speed to high and blend for another 20-30 seconds. Sprinkle a little more thyme on top if you like.

gazpacho

Like its French cousin Vichyssoise, Gazpacho is a chilled
soup from Spain. Not only is it cool and refreshing,
it's packed with energy-boosting nutrients feeding body
and spirit.

ingredients

60ml (3½fl oz) tomato juice
1 tomato, peeled, de-seeded and chopped
1 apple, cored and chopped
¼ cucumber, peeled and chopped
1 spring onion (scallion) chopped finely
1 quarter clove of garlic, chopped finely (optional)
chopped coriander

method

Put the tomato, tomato juice, chopped apple and cucumber
into the blender with the spring onion, garlic and coriander. Blend
on a low speed for around 20 seconds. Gradually (if possible)
increase the speed to high and blend for another 20-30 seconds.

vegetable smoothies **95**

fennel cream

Fennel is a bulb-like vegetable, similar to celery, and an excellent source of Vitamin A. It has a distinctly anise taste, tempered here with the coconut milk in a sort of vegetable pastis!

ingredients

100ml (3½fl oz) coconut milk (see recipe on page 29)
100g (about 3½oz) of chopped fresh Florence fennel
1 apple, peeled, cored and chopped
1 pinch of fennel seeds

method

In a blender, combine the coconut milk, chopped Florence fennel, chopped apple and fennel seeds and blend on a low speed for around 20 seconds. Gradually (if possible) increase the speed to high and blend for another 20-30 seconds.

avocado, tomato & coriander

This smoothie is described as 'guacamole in a glass'.
Avocados started life in Peru where they were first cultivated
some 9,000 years ago. Rich in potassium, a lack of which can
lead to depression and exhaustion, they are a high-protein,
high-energy and high protection-factor food.

ingredients

1 avocado*   fresh coriander
2 tomatoes

method

Peel and de-stone the avocado. Wash and chop the tomatoes
and chop some coriander. Combine all the ingredients in a
blender and blend together. Garnish with a sprig of coriander.
Alternatively, sprinkle with a little chopped chive or spring onion
(scallion) for extra bite and Vitamin A.

* If you have a latex (rubber) allergy, you have a 50% chance of
being allergic to avocados.

green peace

Most of us would shrink at the very thought of drinking cabbage juice but this is a surprisingly mild-flavoured smoothie. Curly kale is probably the tastiest member of the cabbage family and its dark green leaves, which are packed with Vitamin A and chlorophyll, are an indicator of its beneficial properties: it moves vital oxygen to the body's tissues which helps to release the energy stored in foods.

ingredients

4 broccoli florets, chopped

1 small handful of curly kale leaves, chopped

1 small celery stalk, chopped

1 apple, peeled cored and chopped, or use a good splash of apple juice

method

Place the broccoli, curly kale, celery and apple (or apple juice) into the blender and blend on a slow speed until smooth. Gradually increase the speed to high and blend for a further 20-30 seconds.

vichyssoise à la vitesse

Vichyssoise is normally served chilled, but I find this thick, smooth soup-drink is most flavourful straight from the blender.

ingredients

100ml (3½fl oz) vegetable stock
100 (3½fl oz)ml milk/soya milk/tofu
1 spring onion (scallion) chopped
2-3 small cooked potatoes, chopped
1 tsp fresh parsley, chopped
salt and pepper to taste

method

Put the vegetable stock, milk, onion and cooked potatoes into the blender. Sprinkle in the parsley and blend on a low speed for around 20 seconds. Gradually (if possible) increase the speed to high and blend for another 20-30 seconds. Season to taste.

vegetable smoothies **99**

watercress & pear

Watercress is a member of the health-giving *Cruciferae* family of vegetables which includes cabbages, broccoli, sprouts, kale, turnips and horseradish. A rich source of Vitamins A, C and E, watercress is a powerful weapon in the battle against cancer and cardiovascular disease.

ingredients

2 ripe pears, cored and chopped, or use canned fruit
1 handful of watercress, chopped

method

Combine the watercress and the pears in the blender by blending on a low speed for around 20 seconds. Gradually (if possible) increase the speed to high and blend for another 20-30 seconds.

garlic gargle

Harness the healing powers of garlic in this mix: garlic inhibits cancer-cell production and protects the vital organs from damage inflicted by synthetic drugs, radiation and pollution. It also lowers LDL cholesterol and reduces blood-clotting, thereby reducing the risk of blocked arteries and heart disease. If you are worried about your breath afterwards, take heart: parsley is Nature's breath freshener and it's one of the richest sources of vitamin C!

ingredients

4 carrots, cooked and chopped, or one can of carrots, or 125ml (4fl oz) carrot juice
1-2 cloves garlic, chopped
3 sprigs of parsley, chopped

method

Place the chopped garlic, the cooked carrots and the chopped parsley into the blender. Blend on a low speed for around 20 seconds. Gradually (if possible) increase the speed to high and blend for another 20-30 seconds.

coriander-pear

Boost your body's circulation with this mild-tasting mix of pear, carrot and fresh coriander. Coriander is rich in minerals and volatile oils and for centuries has been used in Ayurvedic medicine as a diuretic and antispasmodic.

ingredients

2 pears, fresh or canned, chopped

2 carrots, cooked, or a small can of carrots

1 small handful of coriander, chopped

method

Combine the chopped pears, cooked carrots and chopped coriander in the blender. Blend on a low speed for around 20 seconds. Gradually (if possible) increase the speed to high and blend for another 20-30 seconds.

sunny

A great breakfast juice: it's the colour of the sun and packed full of vitamins and minerals to get your morning kick-started. The betacarotene in the carrots is converted in the body into Vitamin A, which helps to protect the skin from harmful UV rays.

ingredients

1 apple, cored and chopped
2 carrots, cooked and chopped, or a small can of carrots
1 orange, peeled and broken into segments

method

Put the chopped apple, the cooked carrots and the orange in the blender and blend on a low speed for around 20 seconds. Gradually (if possible) increase the speed to high and blend for another 20-30 seconds.

mr green

With its high Vitamin E content, broccoli is one of the best 'skin improvers' around. At the same time, the ellagic acids in grapes deactivate carcinogens, the flavinoids protect the heart while the boron helps to maintain oestrogen levels and thus prevent calcium loss. Remember, 'you are what you eat', so be a natural beauty – inside and out!

ingredients

150g (about 5oz) grapes – either red or green or both – or you can use grape juice

4-5 small broccoli florets

method

Place the grapes or grape juice into the blender with the chopped broccoli florets and blend on a slow speed until well mixed. Gradually increase the speed to high and blend for a further 20-30 seconds.

carrot, orange & coriander

Carrot and orange make a terrific mix. Coriander is a very aromatic herb: in India it is one of the most popular food plants with its fresh leaves sprinkled liberally over curries. Ayurvedic physicians have for centuries used coriander as a digestive aid and to enhance male potency!

ingredients

2 carrots, cooked and chopped, or 100ml (3½fl oz) carrot juice
1 orange, peeled and broken into segments
small bunch of fresh coriander

method

Put the carrots and the orange in the blender with the chopped coriander and blend on a low speed for around 20 seconds. Gradually (if possible) increase the speed to high and blend for another 20-30 seconds.

italia

Basil is reputed among herbalists to be a mood enhancer, but it is also antiseptic and used widely across the Mediterranean for treating headaches, back and rheumatic pains. It is the perfect accompaniment to juicy, ripe tomatoes in a mix that combines the favourite flavours of Italy.

ingredients

½ small bunch fresh basil, chopped finely

2 tomatoes, peeled, de-seeded and chopped or (60ml/ 2fl oz) tomato juice

100ml (3½fl oz) natural, live yoghurt (see recipe on page 31)

dash of balsamic vinegar

dash of olive oil

black pepper to taste

method

Chop the basil and combine in the blender with the tomatoes, yoghurt, oil and vinegar. Blend on a low speed for around 20 seconds. Gradually (if possible) increase the speed to high and blend for another 20-30 seconds. Sprinkle a little fresh, ground black pepper on top.

papaya & carrot

Papayas are native to Costa Rica and southern Mexico and were called 'tree melons' by Christopher Columbus. Both papayas and carrots are packed with betacarotene, so this smoothie is a terrific way to protect your skin from the dangerous UV rays of the sun.

ingredients

2 medium-sized carrots, cooked, or a can of cooked carrots, or 100ml (3½fl oz) carrot juice

1 small papaya, fresh or canned

squeeze of lime juice

method

Put the carrots, the papaya and the lime juice into the blender. Blend on a low speed for around 20 seconds. Gradually (if possible) increase the speed to high and blend for another 20-30 seconds.

3 c's

Cucumbers started life in southern Asia and became popular in ancient Egypt, Greece and Rome for their refreshing and clean flavour. Oddly though, cucumbers have very little nutritional value beyond a tiny amount of Vitamin A, which is good for the skin and eyes and traces of iodine. But because of their high water content, they are low in calories and very refreshing and the carrots and spicy watercress more than compensate for what the cucumber lacks!

ingredients

½ cucumber, peeled, de-seeded and chopped
2 carrots, cooked, or small can of carrots, or 100ml (3½fl oz) of carrot juice
handful of watercress, chopped

method

Combine the ingredients in the blender blending on a low speed to begin with and gradually increasing to a high speed for about 20 seconds or so, until smooth.

cucumber cooler

It is the seeds in cucumbers which are probably the most beneficial and it's a sad practice to scoop them out and discard them. The seeds contain sterols which may help the heart by reducing cholesterol. Peppers are high in Vitamins A and C and also contain some potassium, making them, like tomatoes, antioxidant, anticancer and 'heart protectors'.

ingredients

½ cucumber, peeled, de-seeded (if you must!) and chopped
1 tomato or about 60ml (2fl oz) tomato juice
½ green pepper, de-seeded and chopped
chopped dill

method

Combine the cucumber, tomato and the pepper in the blender with some chopped dill. Blend on a low speed for around 20 seconds. Gradually (if possible) increase the speed to high and blend for another 20-30 seconds. Sprinkle a little chopped dill on top.

sage wisdom

This evergreen shrub with its wrinkled grey-green leaves is native to the western USA and Mexico. Its volatile oil kills bacteria and fungi, even those that are resistant to penicillin! Avoid sage if you are breast-feeding, as it inhibits breast-milk production. But if you are suffering hot flushes and night sweats during the menopause, then sage is for you!

ingredients

100ml (3½fl oz) beetroot juice

1 tbsp lemon juice

2 tbsp cooked, chopped beetroot

1 apple, cored and chopped

small bunch chopped, fresh sage leaves

method

In the blender, combine the beetroot juice, the lemon juice, the cooked chopped beetroot, chopped apple and sage. Blend on a low speed for around 20 seconds. Gradually (if possible) increase the speed to high and blend for another 20-30 seconds.

turmeric cocktail

Turmeric is a member of the ginger family and is native to southeast Asia. The long rhizome looks a little like ginger, but it is rounder and thinner and has a brilliant orange flesh. The dried root, which is ground for use, is a veritable elixir of goodness: antioxidant anti-inflammatory, antibacterial, anti-fungal, anti-viral, anticoagulant, pain-reducing, lowers cholesterol, and is also anticancer.

ingredients

60ml (2fl oz) carrot juice, or a small can of carrots
60ml (2fl oz) tomato juice
1 tomato, peeled, de-seeded and chopped

1 small celery stalk, chopped
1 teaspoon ground turmeric
pinch crushed celery seeds
chopped dill

method

Put the carrot juice (or canned carrots), tomato juice, chopped tomato, celery, the herbs, seeds and turmeric into the blender. Blend on a low speed for around 20 seconds. Gradually (if possible) increase the speed to high and blend for another 20-30 seconds.

snoozey smoothie

In the *Tale of Peter Rabbit* by Beatrix Potter, crisp, juicy lettuce was what caused the eponymous hero to fall asleep in Mr McGregor's garden. Celery was the choice of treatment for 'nervous patients' by the father of modern medicine, Hippocrates. The combined sedative effects of lettuce, the calming effects of celery and the tryptophan released by the body when carbohydrate is digested, ensure a good night's sleep!

ingredients

3 celery stalks, chopped

½ small lettuce, chopped – the more dark green the leaves the better!

½ cucumber, peeled and de-seeded, chopped

method

Place all the ingredients in the blender and blend on a low speed for 20 seconds or so. Increase the speed and blend for a further 20 seconds or so until smooth.

popeye's punch

This mix has become something of a contemporary classic 'cocktail'. It's not surprising, as it really is a great way to 'eat your greens' without noticing! Spinach is source of Vitamin A, and, while it does contain a little iron, is also higher in protein than most other vegetables! The bioflavinoids found in the pith and the segment walls of citrus fruit help to strengthen the walls of tiny blood capillaries and stop the appearance of broken veins on the surface of the skin. One of the merits of blending as opposed to juicing, is that you use the complete fruit – vitamins, minerals and fibre too!

ingredients

2 oranges, peeled and broken into segments
6 spinach leaves, chopped

method

Peel the oranges and break them into segments. Chop the spinach and place it in the blender with the oranges. Blend on a low speed for around 20 seconds. Gradually (if possible) increase the speed to high and blend for another 20-30 seconds.

green tea smoothie

Green tea (*Camellia sinensis*) is indigenous to the wet forests of Asia and is now grown commercially across the world. It is antioxidant and a diuretic and researchers have recently found it to contain anticancer agents. It does, however, contain caffeine, so limit your intake if you have any health conditions aggravated by caffeine.

ingredients

100ml (about 3fl oz) green tea infusion: 2 tsp dried green tea leaves steeped for 10 minutes in 100ml (3fl oz) boiling water and then allowed to cool

60g (2oz) green or white grapes, cut in half

60g (2oz) blueberries or blackberries fresh, frozen or canned

1 sprig of parsley, chopped

method

Make up the green tea infusion and allow it to cool. When ready, place the green tea infusion into the blender along with the grapes and berries and the chopped parsley. Blend on a low speed for around 20 seconds. Gradually (if possible) increase the speed to high and blend for another 20-30 seconds.

leafy lunch

This mix has a peppery and herby bite, brought to it by the dark green leaves of watercress. Hippocrates recognised the value of watercress in 460 BC: he built his 'hospital' next to a stream so he could grow it, while in the 1920s, the British Admiralty gave sailors tablets made from dried watercress to keep scurvy at bay.

ingredients

2 apples, cored and chopped (or 60ml/2fl oz of apple juice)
125g (4oz) green grapes (or 60ml/2fl oz white grape juice)
25g/1oz watercress, chopped
a few sprigs of coriander, chopped
½ lime, squeezed

method

Place all the ingredients into the blender and blend on a low speed for around 20 seconds. Gradually (if possible) increase the speed to high and blend for another 20-30 seconds.

dill-lightful

In the 18th and 19th centuries, children were given dill seeds, known commonly as 'meting seeds', to chew on in church to keep them quiet during long sermons! Cucumber is a terrific internal 'rinse' because of its high water content.

ingredients

1 small bunch of dill

½ cucumber peeled, de-seeded and chopped into chunks

1 large tomato, peeled, de-seeded and chopped, or 60ml (2fl oz) tomato juice

1 carrot, cooked and chopped, or ½ small can carrots, chopped or 60ml (2fl oz) carrot juice

black pepper to taste

method

Strip the fronds of dill from the stalks and chop the leaves. Peel and de-seed the cucumber and tomato and then chop. Cook and chop the carrot. Put the ingredients into the blender and blend for 20 seconds on a low speed. Check for seasoning, adding a little black pepper if needed, and then blend again on a high speed for 15-20 seconds.

chilled-out chilli

Chilli peppers, together with pimento and sweet peppers, are all members of the *Capsicum* family, native to the Americas and introduced to Europe by Christopher Columbus. Native North Americans have used peppers for more than 5,000 years as food and medicine. Powerful antioxidants, chillis are beneficial against age-related macular degeneration (AMD).

ingredients

1 red chilli pepper – if you want a milder smoothie, then remove the seeds before chopping

2 tomatoes (or about 60ml/2fl oz tomato juice)

2 carrots, cooked and chopped, or use a can of carrots, or about 80-100ml (3-3½fl oz) carrot juice

crushed ice

method

Chop the chilli, peel and chop the tomatoes, cook and chop the carrots. Blend on a low speed for around 20 seconds. Gradually (if possible) increase the speed to high and blend for another 20-30 seconds. Pour the mix into a glass two-thirds filled with crushed ice.

a-ok

Alliums (onions) are the OK ingredients in this super antioxidant cocktail. Onions have been used for centuries across the continents for both food and medicine, for making delicious French Onion Soup, and for warding off plague! Onions are Nature's cure-all and are especially effective for the circulatory system.

ingredients

¼ onion, peeled and chopped *cooked gently to soften if prefered
¼-½ garlic clove, chopped
1 apple, cored and chopped
2 carrots, cooked and chopped, or a small can of carrots, or 100ml (3½fl oz) carrot juice
1 big sprig of parsley

method

Place all the ingredients except the parsley into the blender and blend on a low speed for around 20 seconds. Gradually (if possible) increase the speed to high and blend for another 20-30 seconds. After drinking, chew on the parsley — it's Nature's very own breath-freshener!

joint juice

Because leeks are diuretic and have the ability to eliminate uric acid, they can be helpful if you suffer from aching joints or arthritis. They can be a bit 'gritty', so clean them thoroughly before use. Don't discard too much of the dark green leaf at the top as this is a great source of betacarotene which the body converts into Vitamin A.

ingredients

2 leeks, chopped and steamed to soften if preferred

2 carrots, cooked and chopped, or can of carrots, or about 125ml (4fl oz) carrot juice

3 sprigs of parsley

method

Combine the leeks and the carrots in the blender with 2 of the sprigs of parsley and blend on a low speed for around 20 seconds. Gradually (if possible) increase the speed to high and blend for another 20-30 seconds. After drinking, chew on the third sprig of parsley to refresh your mouth after the peppery leeks.

dairy & dairy alternative smoothies

Making smoothies with milk, yoghurt, tofu or fortified soya milk is a really great way to add bone-building calcium and protein into your diet. These are vital for the growth and maintenance of bones and tissues in people of all ages, not just children and post-menopausal women!

Milk is a good source of Vitamins B and D, and this is true not just of whole (full-fat) milk, but of skimmed (reduced-fat) milks too. All of the recipes can be made using full, skimmed or semi-skimmed milk, or full or half-fat evaporated milk.

Buttermilk is a by-product of the butter-making process. It's a rich, creamy liquid with a natural bite. It doesn't contain any butter though! Using it in smoothies makes for a really nice texture with less fat than whole milk. You can now buy dried/powdered buttermilk as well as the more familiar dried cow's milk: both are convenient and easy to use and are an economical alternative to fresh milk. All you have to do is make up the dried milk with water to the quantity required and use it instead of fresh milk in the recipe.

Yoghurt is a fermented milk product which contains beneficial bacteria called lactobacillus which help to maintain the balance of 'gut flora' in the intestinal tract. Oddly, many people who can't tolerate milk find that they can digest yoghurt. You can buy ready-made yoghurts very easily, and in different flavours if you want them, but make sure you buy live yoghurts, with active bacterial cultures and wherever possible, products free from added preservatives and colourings. You can also get soya yoghurts and goat's and ewe's milk yoghurts which can be used in place of milk to make a thicker, creamier smoothie. If you want to make your own live, natural yoghurt, it's very easy to do. Just look at the recipe on page 31.

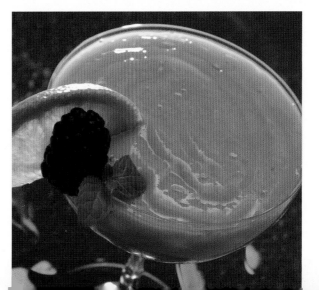

Increasingly, many people find that they are unable to tolerate cow's milk and dairy products. Thankfully, there is now a readily available range of alternatives which are stocked by supermarkets at reasonable prices. These alternatives include non-dairy soya milk and rice milk, as well as goat's and ewe's milk and yoghurt. If you have a lactose intolerance then you can substitute any of these for the dairy milk in the recipes. Soya milk contains more protein and iron but less fat and fewer calories than cow's milk. It has no cholesterol, but only about one-fifth of the amount of calcium of cow's milk (which is why many soya milks on the market are fortified with extra calcium). Rice milk is made from brown and white rice and filtered water. When fortified, it provides as much calcium and Vitamins A and D as cow's milk. It's also very low in fat and contains no lactose at all, so is perfect if you are lactose intolerant. Soya milk and rice milk can be used in any of the recipes in place of dairy milk.

You can freeze milk and yoghurt of all kinds in ice cube trays, and the crushed cubes can be used in smoothies.

There are other 'milks' which can be made from fruit and nuts and are a surprisingly rich source of the protein and calcium we associate with dairy foods. These milks are made by combining chopped dried fruits or unsalted nuts with boiling water. Low in fat and cholesterol, you can use them in place of milk in any smoothie recipe. Because of the concentration of sugars in dried fruit, fruit milks are themselves sweet. On the other hand, nut milks can be used to cut the natural sweetness of fruit smoothies and make for slightly thicker shakes and smoothies than soya milk or juices. In all the recipes, you can substitute a nut milk for the milk, stated. If you look at pages 30-1, you will find the recipes for some fruit and nut milks. Do be aware, though, that if you have a nut allergy, you are also likely to be allergic to a nut milk.

banana & orange smoothie

Mild and fresh, this a real smooth way to start the day. You'll get the Vitamin C of the orange along with hesperidum and limonene in the pith – and slow-release sugar from the banana to sustain your energy levels.

ingredients

1 orange, peeled and broken in segments

2 small bananas or one large one!

100ml (3½fl oz) or more, natural live yoghurt (see recipe on page 31)

method

Peel the banana and break into chunks. Peel the orange and break into segments. Put the fruit into the blender and blend until smooth. Add the yoghurt and blend again. Turn the blender up to high speed and blend for 15-20 seconds until smooth and frothy.

full tank

This really is 'breakfast in a glass', and makes a good 300ml (½ pint) serving. You can use fresh pineapple, or substitute with canned fruit, but make sure it's in its own juice, not in sugary syrup. Again, if you don't have a juicer to tackle the apple, you can still whizz it in a blender/food processor, or even use a dash of ready made juice, organic of course!

ingredients

¼ pineapple, or about 100g (3½ oz) of canned pineapple in its own juice

1 small apple, or a good dash of ready-made, pressed organic apple juice

100ml (3½fl oz) soya milk

1 small handful of alfalfa sprouts

ice cube

method

Remove the skin from the pineapple, if using fresh, and wash, core and chop the apple. Place the fruit and the alfalfa sprouts in the blender/food processor and blend until smooth. Add the soya milk and ice cube and blend again briefly. Serve in a tall glass and sprinkle a few alfalfa sprouts on top to garnish.

get up and go!

A wonderful sweet-sour mix of orange and prune. A pun is intended, albeit a bad one since everyone knows the properties of prunes, but did you know that the Vitamin C in the oranges helps the body to absorb the iron in the prunes? This combination is excellent if you are run down or anaemic, so you really can 'get up and go!'

ingredients

6 prunes (de-stoned), chopped

2 oranges, peeled, or 100ml (3½fl oz) freshly squeezed orange juice

2 tbsp natural, live yoghurt (for recipe, see page 31)

pinch ground cinnamon

method

Place the prunes, oranges (or orange juice) and yoghurt together in a blender/food processor. Blend on a low speed for around 20 seconds. Gradually (if possible) increase the speed to high and blend for another 20-30 seconds. Pour into a glass and sprinkle with a pinch of cinnamon.

wake-up call

If absolutely nothing but coffee will get you up and at it in the morning, then try this delicious, spicy iced coffee. It's especially good in summer, but is also a nice way to enjoy a midday or post-lunch coffee!

ingredients

½ tbsp freshly ground coffee
½ tsp ground nutmeg
½ tsp ground cardamom
250ml (½ pint) boiling water
1 tbsp vanilla ice cream
½ tbsp honey
ice cubes
sprinkle of cardamom to garnish

method

Put the coffee, nutmeg and cardamom into a heatproof bowl and pour on the boiling water. Leave to stand until cold. Strain into blender/food processor and blend with ice cream and honey. Pour into a glass over ice cubes and sprinkle with a little ground cardamom.

mandarin & lychee smoothie

The bright red, rough skin of the lychee hides a sweet-acid flesh like a grape beneath it. Lychees are a great source of Vitamins B and C and are good for the digestion, which is why they are often served after a Chinese meal.

ingredients

100g (4oz) lychees, peeled (canned are ok too, but drain and wash them if in syrup)
3 mandarins or satsumas/clementines
100ml (3½fl oz) natural, live yoghurt (for recipe, see page 31)
pinch of ground ginger

method

Peel the lychees and mandarins and put them into a blender/food processor with the yoghurt. Blend on a low speed for around 20 seconds. Gradually (if possible) increase the speed to high and blend for another 20-30 seconds. Pour into a glass and dust with a sprinkle of ground ginger.

smooth passion

A really pronounced passion fruit flavour — something to be savoured slowly! The sweet, golden flesh of passion fruits has many black but edible seeds that can't be separated unless you strain the fruit — but then you will lose the many minerals they contain!

ingredients

2 passion fruits

1 small banana

1 orange

200ml (7fl oz) natural, live yoghurt (for recipe, see page 31)

method

Cut the passion fruits in half and scoop out the flesh. Peel and break the banana into chunks. Peel and break the orange into segments. Place all the fruit into the blender with the yoghurt. Blend on a low speed for around 20 seconds. Gradually (if possible) increase the speed to high and blend for another 20-30 seconds.

cucumber raita

Cucumber and yoghurt combine to create the cooling properties that balance the hotness of Indian curries. Even without the curry, this drink is a refreshing reviver, with the added benefits of being low in calories, but beneficial to the immune system.

ingredients

¼ cucumber, peeled and diced, and a couple of slices for garnish

60ml (2fl oz) natural live yoghurt (for recipe, see page 31)

60ml (2fl oz) milk

10-12 mint leaves and a sprig reserved for garnish

squeeze of lime juice

pinch of salt to taste

ice cubes

method

Put the diced cucumber into a blender/food processor with the yoghurt, milk and mint. Blend on a low speed for around 20 seconds. Gradually (if possible) increase the speed to high and blend for another 20-30 seconds. Pour into a glass half filled with ice. Garnish with a sprig of mint.

apricot & apple whey

The whey that Little Miss Muffet was eating alongside her curds, is the liquid and the 'soft cheese' left over when making hard cheeses such as Cheddar. Whey contains valuable lactic acid and proteins.

ingredients

4 fresh apricots (or 3-4 dried apricots rehydrated by cooking in a little water till plump, then cooled and drained)

1 apple (or 60ml/2fl oz apple juice)

100ml (3½fl oz) whey, buttermilk or natural live yoghurt (for recipe, see page 31)

method

Wash and stone the apricots, then chop into pieces. Wash the apple, core and chop into pieces. Put the fruit pieces into the blender and blend on a low speed for around 20 seconds. Gradually (if possible) increase the speed to high and blend for another 20-30 seconds. Pour in the whey or yoghurt, blending again briefly. Pour into a glass and garnish with a little apricot.

green goddess

Avocado to boost your energy, dill to calm the stomach, chives to cleanse the system and natural, live yoghurt to boost your 'good bacteria' levels in the gut and to lift your spirits. Because yoghurt synthesises some of the B Vitamins, it helps to prevent those low periods when you feel 'blue'.

ingredients

1 avocado
100ml (3½fl oz) natural, live yoghurt (for recipe, see page 31)
fresh dill
fresh chives
seasoning to taste
mineral water (optional)

method

Chop some chives and dill leaves finely. Peel and de-stone the avocado and chop the flesh. Purée the avocado and herbs with the yoghurt in a food processor/blender until smooth. Season to taste. If a little too thick, add a splash of mineral water. Pour into a glass and sprinkle a few chopped herbs on top.

mango smoothie

A really reviving drink with a slight tang of lime. If you can't find, or don't want to use, rice milk, try it with natural, live yoghurt instead.

ingredients

1 ripe mango
squeeze of lime juice
250ml or so (about ½ pint) rice milk
fresh mint or lemon balm to garnish

method

Peel and remove the flesh from the mango. Put the flesh into a food processor/blender and add a squeeze of lime juice. Pour in the rice milk and blend together on a low speed until smooth. Pour into a glass and garnish with the sprig of lemon balm or mint.

banana & date energiser

'Candy that grows on trees' is how dates have been described. Fresh or dried, they are excellent energy snacks: they are 75-80% all-natural sugars, high in carbohydrate and food energy. They also contain potassium, calcium, magnesium as well as small amounts of Vitamins A, B complex, and C.

ingredients

150ml (about ¼ pint) live natural yoghurt (for recipe, see page 31)
1 small ripe banana
3 dried dates with stones removed
Pinch of ground cinnamon to garnish

method

Peel the banana and de-stone the dates. Cut the fruit into chunks and place in a blender/food processor with the yoghurt and blend on a low speed until smooth. Dust with a sprinkle of ground cinnamon.

the white stuff

If you can't find buttermilk, remember you can always substitute natural, live yoghurt. This energiser has the added bonus of a little (note 'little'!) grated chocolate on top, and why not? Sometimes, nothing else except chocolate will do to give you a real boost. Chocolate is rich in phenylethylamine, the same substance manufactured by the brain when you are in love!

ingredients

1 kiwi fruit

1 small banana

1 small apple (or 60ml/2fl oz apple juice)

150ml (3½fl oz) buttermilk, or natural live yoghurt (for recipe, see page 31)

lightly chilled mineral water

a little grated chocolate

method

Wash, core and chop the apple. Peel the kiwi and banana, reserving a slice of each for garnish. Purée the kiwi, apple and banana and blend in the buttermilk or yoghurt. Stir in a little mineral water if you like, pour into a glass and garnish with a little grated chocolate.

vitaliser

A lovely blend of banana, blueberries and nectarine in a smooth yoghurt. Blueberries contain the antibacterial anthocyanosides which have a toning effect on the blood, while nectarines are ideal for anyone with high cholesterol levels, or blood pressure problems.

ingredients

1 small ripe banana

50g (1¾oz) blueberries

1 nectarine

1 small ripe pear

100ml (3½oz) live natural yoghurt (for recipe, see page 31)

splash of mineral water (optional)

method

Peel the banana, wash the blueberries, wash and remove the stalk and core from the pear and wash and de-stone the nectarine. Keep a few berries for garnish. Put the fruit into the blender and blend on a low speed for around 20 seconds. Gradually (if possible) increase the speed to high and blend for another 20-30 seconds. Stop the machine and pour in the yoghurt and blend again briefly until well mixed.

pick-me-up

The Aztecs though that chocolate was the food of the gods. A little chocolate will perk you up and bring a smile to your face because it contains phenylethylamine, the chemical produced by the brain when we fall in love!

ingredients

1 small ripe banana
100ml (3½fl oz) live, natural yoghurt (for recipe, see page 31)
1 orange, squeezed or juiced
a little grated chocolate

method

In a blender/food processor, purée the banana with the yoghurt and mix in the juice of the orange. Pour into a glass and dust with some grated chocolate. If you need an extra lift, add a teaspoon of honey into the blend.

chocolate shake

Introduced to Europe by Christopher Columbus, surprisingly, it took more than 100 years for us to become 'addicted' to chocolate! Sometimes, nothing else will do. Yes, you could use carob, or St John's Bread as it is called since the Baptist managed in the wilderness on wild honey and locusts. When slowly roasted, the leguminous pods of carob are supposed to taste something like chocolate.

ingredients

6 squares of chocolate:
   use chocolate with a high
   cocoa content
2 scoops chocolate ice cream

250ml (about ½ pint) full-fat
   (whole) milk
whipped cream to decorate

method

Grate the chocolate or melt it in a bowl over a saucepan of hot water. Put the milk, the chocolate and the ice cream into a food processor/blender and blend until the desired thickness is reached. You can, at this stage throw in a banana or a few berries too! Pour into a tall glass, and decorate with a good dollop of whipped cream.

buttermilkshake

Real buttermilk can be hard to find, although some health and whole food stores do sell it when they can source it. It is a natural by-product of butter churned from raw, unpasteurised cream. (Cultured buttermilk is pasteurised skim-milk inoculated with a lactic acid culture and then incubated.) Thicker than regular milk, buttermilk, in spite of its name, is actually lower in fat.

ingredients

100ml (3½fl oz) buttermilk or natural, live yoghurt (for recipe, see page 31)

¼ small pineapple or 3 sliced canned fruit

75g (2½oz) grapes

1 vanilla pod

ground cinnamon

method

Purée the pineapple and grapes in a food processor/blender. Mix in the buttermilk or yoghurt. Slit the vanilla pod in half lengthways and scrape out the seeds with the point of a knife. Add them to the buttermilk/yoghurt mix and stir well. Pour into a large glass and garnish with a sprinkle of ground cinnamon.

banana-fig

Figs are positively bursting with natural food energy: 55% sugars, they will give you a natural 'high' and provide carbohydrate, fibre and even a small amount of protein. Calcium, magnesium, phosphorous and potassium are all found in abundant levels found in figs.

ingredients

1 banana

1 fresh fig

100ml (3½fl oz) buttermilk,
  of live natural yoghurt (for
  recipe, see page 31)

½ vanilla pod

100ml (3½fl oz) sparkling
  mineral water

ground cinnamon

ice cubes

method

Chop the banana into chunks. Cut open the fig and scoop out the flesh. Put the banana, fig and buttermilk, or live natural yoghurt, into a blender/food processor and blend until smooth. Cut a vanilla pod in half lengthwise and scrape out half of the seeds with the point of a knife and add them to the mixture. Blend briefly again. Pour into a glass over ice cubes and top with sparkling mineral water. Dust with a sprinkle of ground cinnamon.

raspberry buttermilk

This needs a little bit of preparation in advance, but it's well worth it! If you don't want to make frozen grape juice cubes, you can use a few frozen raspberries instead.

ingredients

40g (about 1oz white grapes or 30ml (about fl oz) white grape juice
75g (2½oz) raspberries
1 pear
100ml (3½fl oz) buttermilk, or live natural yoghurt (for recipe, see page 31)
chilled mineral water

method

Pour the grape juice into an ice cube tray and freeze for about 4 hours. Put the pear, the raspberries and the buttermilk, or live natural yoghurt, in a blender/food processor and blend until smooth. If too thick, dilute with a little chilled mineral water. Put the grape cubes into a glass and pour over the buttermilk, or live natural yoghurt-shake.

banana & coconut milk

In the battle against stress, Vitamins B and C and the minerals zinc, potassium, calcium, magnesium and iron are important. Bananas and coconuts are both foods known to have a very calming effect on the nerves, while spices such as cinnamon and ginger are also well-known as great stress-relievers.

ingredients

2 large ripe bananas

250ml (about ½ pint) coconut milk

pinch of ground cinnamon

method

Put the coconut milk and the bananas into a blender/food processor and blend until smooth. Pour into a glass and sprinkle with a pinch of ground cinnamon.

banana calmer

Soothe your mind and nourish nerves after a stressful day at work. The fibre in the banana helps lower cholesterol, while potassium is a great relaxer and 'cramp beater'!

ingredients

250ml (½ pint) milk

1 banana, peeled and sliced

2-3 ice cubes

1 tsp honey

1 pinch ground or fresh grated nutmeg

method

Put all the ingredients into a blender/food processor and blend on a low speed for around 20 seconds. Gradually (if possible) increase the speed to high and blend for another 20-30 seconds. Serve with a pinch of nutmeg on top.

smooth serenity

Nourishing and calming, this sweet blend with a hint of spice will help stabilise the nerves and help you to concentrate. Almonds are rich in minerals – they have the most of all nuts – as well as zinc, magnesium, potassium and iron.

ingredients

½ tbsp ground almonds
100g (4oz) dates, de-stoned
250ml (about ½ pint) rice milk
good pinch ground ginger

method

Put all the ingredients into a blender/food processor and blend on a low speed for around 20 seconds. Gradually (if possible) increase the speed to high and blend for another 20-30 seconds. Serve with a pinch of ground ginger on top, and a few flaked almonds.

pineapple-almond

A delicious way to beat stress and boost your energy levels. Weight for weight, almonds have one-third more protein than eggs! They also have B Vitamins which are vital for nerve function.

ingredients

1 tbsp ground almonds

1 tbsp grated coconut

¼ pineapple, peeled (or 3 thick slices of canned pineapple in own juice, drained)

150ml (3½fl oz) natural live yoghurt (for recipe, see page 31)

method

Purée the almonds and coconut in a blender/food processor with the pineapple. Add the yoghurt and blend again. Pour into a glass and sprinkle with a few flaked almonds.

berry & banana

With their creamy, smooth taste, bananas are a joy to drink. They contain Vitamin B6 and magnesium, and help to keep nerves and muscles healthy. You can use any berry you like in this drink.

ingredients

1 banana
150g (3½oz) berries of your choice
1 tbsp ground almonds
100ml (3½fl oz) buttermilk, or live natural yoghurt (for recipe, see page 31)
mineral water (optional)
pinch ground cinnamon

method

Peel the banana and cut into chunks. Rinse the berries, remove any stalks and pat dry. Keep a few berries aside to garnish. Put the berries and the banana in a blender/food processor along with the ground almonds and buttermilk, or live natural yoghurt. If the mix is too thick, dilute with a splash of mineral water. Season with a pinch of ground cinnamon, pour into a large glass and garnish with the reserved berries.

plum yoghurt

Rich in folic acid, Vitamin C and betacarotene, plums are great for boosting immunity. Folic acid is needed to guard against anaemia and irritability, confusion and memory loss, greying hair and gastrointestinal disorders, all the tangible signs of stress!

ingredients

4 plums, de-stoned
100ml (3½oz) natural live yoghurt (for recipe, see page 31)
1 apple
mineral water (optional)
pinch ground cinnamon

method

Wash and de-stone the plums. Wash the apple and chop into chunks. Purée the plums and apple in a blender/food processor. Add the yoghurt and blend together. If a little too thick, add a dash or two of mineral water. Pour into a glass and sprinkle with ground cinnamon.

heights of passion

A good source of Vitamins A and C, the punchy flavour of passion fruit is hard to resist. Don't worry about the seeds, they're edible too! Mixed with yoghurt into a smoothie, it's a really 'posh pudding'!

ingredients

2 passion fruits
1 orange
½ lime
100ml (3½ oz) natural live yoghurt (for recipe, see page 31)
sparkling mineral water (optional)

method

Scoop the flesh from the passion fruits, squeeze the orange and lime, or simply peel and pop in a blender/food processor along with the passion fruit and blend them all together. Add the yoghurt and blend again briefly. Pour into a glass. If you prefer a longer drink, dilute with sparkling mineral water and serve over ice.

papaya & almond dream

Diverticulitis is affecting a growing number of people in the West because of diets rich in highly processed foods, low in fibre and too many caffeinated drinks. A luscious combination of laxative and soothing fruits and anti-inflammatory rice milk can help, as will increasing the amount of exercise taken.

ingredients

6 fresh or 4 dried apricots (re-hydrated by cooking them in a little water until plump, cooled and drained)

¼ papaya, peeled and de-seeded

250ml (½ pint) rice milk

2 tsp ground almonds

pinch of ground or freshly grated ginger

method

Place all the ingredients together in a blender/food processor and blend together until smooth. Pour into a glass and sprinkle with a little ginger.

calmer

The occasional occurrence of diarrhoea can be debilitating and upsetting. It's actually your body trying hard to get rid of something that's upsetting it. Ideally, you should let it 'run its course' if you'll excuse the pun, eliminating the toxins. But you do need to put back fluids and balance the electrolytes in your body too!

ingredients

½ mango, peeled
1 pear, peeled and cored
1 banana
100ml (3½fl oz) rice milk
pinch ground cinnamon

method

Put the mango, pear and banana into a blender/food processor with the rice milk and blend together. Serve with a dusting of ground cinnamon.

avocado calmer

A smooth, creamy drink that should satisfy food cravings,
and for provide relief for those who suffer from PMS.
Avocados are great as they are high in Vitamins B and E
(good for the hormones) and, at the same time, calming
on the nervous system.

ingredients

1 ripe avocado*, peeled and
  sliced
1 clove or garlic, peeled
  (optional)

½ lemon, squeezed
250ml (about ½ pint) rice milk
seasoning to taste
sprig fresh coriander to garnish

method

Put the avocado into a blender/food processor with the garlic clove
(optional), the lemon juice and rice milk and blend until smooth.
Season to taste, pour into a glass and garnish with a sprig of fresh
coriander.

* If you have a latex (rubber) allergy, you have a 50% change of being
allergic to avocados!

raspberry relief

Raspberries are astringent and protect the gut from inflammation. They, like honey, have natural antibiotics, helping to fight off infecting organisms in the gut.

ingredients

100g (4oz) raspberries

2 large tbsp natural, live yoghurt (for recipe, see page 31)

1-2 tsp of honey

2 tbsp milk

method

Put all the ingredients into a blender/food processor and blend together. Pour into a glass. Garnish with a few berries if you like.

thai tango

An exotic combination of tropical fruits, this drink is great for 'reduction' but is also very satisfying – a great way to get those taste buds dancing! The papaya is packed with Vitamin C, betacarotene and enzymes to aid digestion. Pears have a diuretic action to help eliminate toxins and are full of fibre, and the lime helps to clear excess fluids from the body.

ingredients

½ papaya, peeled and de-seeded

1 lime, juiced, keep a slice for garnish

2 pears

150ml (about 5fl oz) rice milk

pinch ground ginger

ice cubes (optional)

method

Cut the papaya flesh into chunks and purée with the juice of the lime in a blender/food processor. Cut the pears into chunks, add these to the mix and purée them too. Pour in the rice milk and blend together until smooth. Pour over ice cubes for a long refreshing drink. Dust with a pinch of ground ginger and garnish with a slice of lime.

apple & apricot smoothie

Apricots are high in fibre and low in calories, but satisfy that urge for something sweet! Apples aid digestion and absorption and have the ability to dampen the appetite, always a bonus when you're keeping an eye on your weight.

ingredients

6 fresh apricots (or 4-5 dried apricots)

2 apples or 60ml (2fl oz) apple juice

100ml (3½fl oz) live natural yoghurt (for recipe, see page 31)

a little freshly grated nutmeg

method

Wash and de-stone the apricots. (If using dried apricots, rehydrate them by covering with water in a saucepan and heating slowly. When plump, allow to cool and drain.) Purée the apricots in a blender/food processor. Wash and chop the apples and add to the purée in the blender/food processor. Mix the fruit purées with the yoghurt. Blend on a low speed for around 20 seconds. Gradually (if possible) increase the speed to high and blend for another 20-30 seconds. Pour into a glass and dust with nutmeg.

cucumber-melon

Melon contains betacarotene, folic acid and minerals such as calcium, choline and magnesium, while cucumber is potassium-rich. Both have diuretic properties and are great detoxers. By adding some natural, live yoghurt, this becomes quite a substantial drink.

ingredients

½ cucumber
½ cantaloupe melon
100ml (3½fl oz) natural, live yoghurt (for recipe, see page 31)
2-3 sprigs of fresh dill
seasoning to taste

method

Wash the dill and strip the leaves from the stalks – save a sprig for garnish if you like. Chop up the rest of the dill very finely. Peel the cucumber and de-seed, and remove the flesh from the melon. In a blender/food processor, purée the cucumber and melon. Sprinkle in the dill, pour in the yoghurt and blend briefly until smooth. Season with pepper to taste. Pour into a tall glass, garnish with the dill or a slice of cucumber.

strawberry shake-up

These summer berries contain bromelaine which helps to 'digest' fat – that's why strawberries go so well with cream! Using yoghurt, which you can make yourself very easily (see page 31), gives a creamy, satisfying texture, so it's nice without being naughty! In summer, try this shake chilled, it's as nice as ice cream and it's full of goodness, too!

ingredients

100g (3oz) strawberries
100ml (3½fl oz) natural live yoghurt (for recipe, see page 31)
50g (1½oz) grapes (red or green) (or 1 small glass of grape juice)
1 orange

method

Wash and hull the strawberries. Put one aside for garnish. Purée the berries, grapes and orange together in a blender/food processor. Add the yoghurt and blend briefly until smooth. Pour into a large glass, and decorate with the strawberry.

apple smoothie

Smoothies made with live natural yoghurt and fresh fruit juices are a great way to start the day and help to maintain the balance of 'good bacteria' in your gut. Whether detoxing or weight-watching, it is vital that your body is nourished. You need to replace vital vitamins and minerals, and energise your body to keep it working efficiently.

ingredients

1 apple, cored and chopped
2 oranges (or 1 small glass of orange juice)
100ml (31/2 fl oz) natural live yoghurt (for recipe, see page ?)
10 small mint leaves, finely chopped

method

Wash, core and chop the apple and peel the oranges. Pour the yoghurt into a blender/food processor and add the fruit. Blend until smooth. Sprinkle with chopped mint leaves and garnish with a slice of orange if you like. If you want a longer drink, add a splash or two of chilled mineral water.

cherry-almond

Cherries are botanically related to peaches, and thereby to almonds too! They are a great source of carbohydrates, contain little fat and protein, and are packed full with vitamins. The only drawback is having to remove the pips: cutting them in half and poking out the pip is one way, but some folks say sticking a (clean) hairpin into the stalk end and pushing the pip out works well!

ingredients

100ml (3½fl oz) almond milk (for recipe, see page 30)
75g (3oz) pitted cherries
75g (3oz) raspberries
⅛ teaspoon (0.5ml/?fl oz) almond extract

method

Put the almond milk, raspberries, pitted cherries and almond extract into the blender and blend on a low speed for around 20 seconds. Gradually (if possible) increase the speed to high and blend for another 20-30 seconds.

peachy almond

Peaches and almonds – a perfect combination, and not surprising as they are, in fact, related to each other as first cousins! Almond milk is easy to make and the recipe is on page 30. Almond extract, often used in baking, is made from bitter almonds – a cousin of the sweet almond nuts we eat and which are also used in cosmetics. In its concentrated form, bitter almond oil is poisonous (it contains prussic acid!) but in the extract, the oil is diluted with water and alcohol.

ingredients

175ml (about 5fl oz) almond milk (for recipe, see page 31)
1 peach (you can use fresh or canned, but drain the liquid off)
4 apricots (fresh, canned or dried)
0.5ml (⅛ tsp) almond extract

method

Put the almond milk, the peaches and apricots in the blender with the almond extract. Blend on a low speed for around 20 seconds. Gradually (if possible) increase the speed to high and blend for another 20-30 seconds until smooth.

baklava

This is a real treat, nutty and sweet at the same time. Sesame seed have, since ancient times, been a staple food: they are the main protein source in many cultures, especially in Africa and the Middle East. The seeds are about 50% fat, mostly unsaturated and about 18% protein. Walnut milk has for centuries been drunk in households that didn't have a cow! Walnuts have a fairly high protein content as well as notable levels of vitamins and minerals.

ingredients

175ml (about 5fl oz) walnut milk (see recipe on page 30)

1 tbsp hulled sesame seeds

1 tbsp (15ml/??fl oz) runny honey

1 peach, fresh or canned

method

Put the walnut milk, sesame seeds, honey and peach into the blender. Blend on a low speed for around 20 seconds. Gradually (if possible) increase the speed to high and blend for another 20-30 seconds.

pina colada

Famous as an alcoholic cocktail, the name means 'strained pineapple', as in parts of the Caribbean it is served in a hollowed-out pineapple. It needs a bit of forward planning, as the ice cubes are made from frozen soya milk, and need to be prepared a little in advance.

ingredients

175ml (about 5fl oz) coconut milk (see recipe on page 29)
3 slices pineapple, chopped, fresh or canned
1 kiwi fruit, chopped
6 frozen soya milk cubes

method

Freeze some soya milk in ice cubes trays in advance. Put the coconut milk, pineapple, kiwi fruit and the soya milk ice cubes into the blender. Blend on a low speed for around 20 seconds. Gradually (if possible) increase the speed to high and blend for another 20-30 seconds until smooth.

dairy & dairy alternative smoothies **159**

peach fuzz

Peaches and apricots are botanically related to each other, but each has its own unique flavour. Both are high in Vitamin A, contain several minerals and are low in fat.

ingredients

100ml (3½fl oz) soya milk
2 oranges, squeezed or 60ml (2fl oz) orange juice
2 peaches, fresh or canned, or 'rehydrate' some dried peaches
2 apricots, fresh or canned, or 'rehydrate' some dried apricots
3-4 ice cubes

method

Wash and de-stone the apricots and peaches. Place the soya milk, the orange (or orange juice) into the blender with the peaches and apricots. (If using dried apricots or peaches, rehydrate them by covering with just enough water in a saucepan and heating slowly. When plump, allow to cool and drain.) Add the ice cubes, one at a time and blend on a low speed for around 20 seconds. Gradually (if possible) increase the speed to high and blend for another 20-30 seconds.

pink lassi

This is a fruity alternative to the classic Lassi, a very popular and refreshing drink from India. This fruit version has a dryness to it that is very refreshing on a hot day! It is also packed with vitamins and minerals to keep you in good health.

ingredients

100ml (3½fl oz) cranberry juice
75g (3oz) raspberries
6 strawberries
100ml (3½fl oz) natural, live yoghurt (for recipe, see page 31)

method

Put the cranberry juice, raspberries and strawberries into the blender with the yoghurt and blend on a low speed for around 20 seconds. Gradually (if possible) increase the speed to high and blend for another 20-30 seconds.

pink cow

Ice cream is a vital ingredient in milkshakes, which are among the earliest blended drinks. Ice cream milkshakes were already popular at the end of the 1700s! Using commercially made ice cream means you are adding extra sugar and extra calories, so keep this for special treats! Alternatively, check out the recipes on pages 181-6 and make up your own blender ice cream and frozen yoghurt.

ingredients

200ml (¼ pint or so) milk
6 strawberries
1 small banana
250ml (2 scoops) strawberry ice cream

method

Combine the milk, strawberries and the banana in the blender and blend until smooth. Add the ice cream and blend on low speed for 20-30 seconds, just until the ice cream is mixed in. You can add more milk to thin, or more ice cream to thicken!

breakfast blitz

Nuts are high in protein, Vitamin E, fibre and protease inhibitors, known to prevent cancer. While high in fat, nut oils are polyunsaturated and help to reduce blood cholesterol levels. As well as vitamin E, wheatgerm is a good source of thiamine, while flax seeds (linseeds) are a great source of essential Omega-3 fatty acids.

ingredients

100ml (3½fl oz) milk, this can be dairy, soya or rice milk
125g (4oz) berries of your choice
1 banana
2 tbsp chopped almonds
2 tbsp wheatgerm
2 tbsp ground flax (linseed) seeds
100ml (3½fl oz) natural, live yoghurt (for recipe, see page 31)

method

Put the milk, berries, chopped almonds, wheatgerm, flax seeds and yoghurt into the blender. Blend on a low speed for around 20 seconds. Gradually (if possible) increase the speed to high and blend for another 20-30 seconds.

spotty smoothie

This is a lovely combination of raspberries and oranges: the flavour of the berries is enhanced by the citric juice of the orange. Raspberries are rich in potassium and niacin and also contain Vitamin C and iron. If you can't find fresh berries, don't forget you can substitute frozen or canned fruits, and if you want to, you can substitute soya yoghurt too!

ingredients

125g (4oz) raspberries, fresh, frozen or canned

2 oranges

100ml (3½fl oz) or more of natural live yoghurt (for recipe, see page 31) or soya yoghurt

method

Peel the oranges and break into segments. Put the oranges and the berries into the blender with the yoghurt. Blend on a low speed for around 20 seconds. Gradually (if possible) increase the speed to high and blend for another 20-30 seconds.

beta blast

All the fruits in this smoothie are prized for their betacarotene, which is converted in the body into Vitamin A. This recipe also makes optional use of silken tofu, soya bean curd, which is an excellent substitute for those with milk allergies.

ingredients

60ml (2fl oz) orange juice
30ml (1fl oz) carrot juice
¼ cantaloupe melon, peeled, de-seeded and chopped
1 apricot, fresh, canned or dried and rehydrated, chopped
30ml (1fl oz) silken tofu (optional)

method

Place the orange and carrot juice in the blender along with the chopped cantaloupe melon and chopped apricots. (If using dried apricots, rehydrate them by covering with just enough water in a saucepan and heating slowly. When plump, allow to cool, then drain and chop.) Add the tofu (if using). Blend on a low speed for around 20 seconds. Gradually (if possible) increase the speed to high and blend for another 20-30 seconds.

moody blue

Blueberries have several names, whortleberry, bilberry, hurtleberry, whinberry, huckleberry and saskatoon! Whatever their name, they are delicious and an antibacterial which makes them terrific for cystitis treatment. Their tonic effect on the blood is also useful in keeping varicose veins at bay! You can use fresh, frozen or canned berries, and if you can't get blueberries, try blackberries instead!

ingredients

75ml (2½fl oz) cranberry-raspberry juice

60g (2oz) blueberries

60ml (2fl oz) red grape juice or a small handful of red grapes!

60ml (2fl oz) silken tofu (or you can use natural, live yoghurt)

method

In a blender, combine the cranberry-raspberry juice, the berries, grapes (or grape juice) and the silken tofu (or yoghurt). Blend on a low speed for around 20 seconds. Gradually (if possible) increase the speed to high and blend for another 20-30 seconds.

nectar smoothie

Nectarines are an ancient fruit and, of course, their juice was the favoured drink of the Greek gods. Fortunately, mere mortals can also enjoy them, and benefit from their antioxidant and anticancer properties.

ingredients

1 nectarine, peeled and chopped

1 orange, peeled and broken into segments

60ml (2fl oz) natural live yoghurt (for recipe, see page 31) or silken tofu

3 ice cubes

method

Place the fruit and the yoghurt into the blender and process until smooth. Drop in the ice cubes, one at a time, and process in short bursts until they are incorporated.

mango & orange smoothie

A gorgeous, silky smooth combination of sweet mango and sharp orange. For more than 4,000 years in their native India, mangoes have been used to treat diabetes and high blood pressure.

ingredients

½ mango fresh or canned
1 orange, peeled and broken into segments
100ml (3½ fl oz) natural, live yoghurt (see recipe on page 31)
squeeze of lime juice

method

Peel and break the orange into segments and chop the mango into pieces. Place in the blender and squeeze on the lime juice. Blend until smooth and then add the yoghurt. Blend on a low speed for around 20 seconds. Gradually (if possible) increase the speed to high and blend for another 20-30 seconds.

peach & lemon yoghurt

Smooth and creamy, you can have this smoothie as thick or as thin as you like. Simply add a splash of mineral water to dilute.

ingredients

2 peaches, fresh or canned in own juice

juice of half a lemon

100ml (3½fl oz) live, natural yoghurt (see recipe on page 31)

method

Halve and stone the peaches if using fresh and cut into chunks. Put them into the blender and squeeze in the lemon juice. Add the yoghurt. Blend on a low speed for around 20 seconds. Gradually (if possible) increase the speed to high and blend for another 20-30 seconds. If too thick, add a splash of mineral water and blend briefly again.

minty pineapple shake

Fresh, ripe pineapple has the most wonderful sweet aroma and taste. When you buy a pineapple, smell its bottom! If it smells sweet and fruity, it's ripe and ready! Mint is a perfect balance to the sweet fruit and it's good for headaches too! This is the perfect pick-me-up after a night of over-indulgence!

ingredients

¼ medium pineapple or 4 thick slices of canned fruit in own juice, drained
100ml (3½ fl oz) natural, live yoghurt (see recipe on page 31)
6 mint leaves, chopped

method

Chop the mint leaves and the pineapple and place in the blender with the yoghurt. Blend on a low speed for around 20 seconds. Gradually (if possible) increase the speed to high and blend for another 20-30 seconds.

pink grapefruit & banana thickie

A power-packed breakfast smoothie that will perk you up and sustain you through the morning. Pink grapefruits are not only a little sweeter than white, they also have more Vitamin C!

ingredients

1 pink grapefruit, peeled and broken into segments
1 banana
100ml (3½fl oz) live, natural yoghurt (see recipe on page 31)

method

Peel the grapefruit and break into segments. Peel the banana and break into chunks. Put the fruit into the blender with the yoghurt and blend on a low speed for around 20 seconds. Gradually (if possible) increase the speed to high and blend for another 20-30 seconds.

blueberry banana

This is just delicious and the blueberries are excellent for the gut. You can use fresh, frozen or dried berries which have been rehydrated by covering with just enough water in a saucepan and heating slowly. When plump, allow to cool and drain. This means you can enjoy these little blue wonders all year round!

ingredients

125g (about 3-4oz) blueberries

1 banana, peeled and chopped

100ml (3½fl oz) or more live, natural yoghurt (for recipe, see page 31)

method

Put the berries and banana in the blender with the yoghurt. Blend on a low speed for around 20 seconds. Gradually (if possible) increase the speed to high and blend for another 20-30 seconds.

avocado shake

Rich in potassium, a lack of which can lead to depression and fatigue, avocados also contain B6 and iron, which are terrific mood enhancers. If you are grumpy in the morning or any time of the day, do something about it and treat yourself with this delicious smoothie.

ingredients

1 avocado*, peeled and stoned

1 grapefruit, peeled and broken into segments

juice of half a lemon

125ml (about 4fl oz) soya milk, rice milk, or natural live yoghurt for a really thick smoothie!

method

Put the avocado, grapefruit and lemon juice into the blender and pour in the soya milk. Blend on a low speed for around 20 seconds. Gradually (if possible) increase the speed to high and blend for another 20-30 seconds.

* If you have a latex (rubber) allergy, you have a 50% change of being allergic to avocados!

nutty date

If you're going to party through the night, you need all the strength you can muster. Dates have a high iron content and plenty of easily converted energy which makes them great 'power-boosters'. The soya milk can be plain, or treat yourself to chocolate flavoured!

ingredients

4 dates, fresh, dried, pitted and chopped

1 apple, cored and chopped

2 tsp chopped almonds

125ml (about 4fl oz) chocolate-flavoured soya milk

method

Chop the dates, core and chop the apple and put in the blender with the chopped almonds. Pour in the chocolate-flavoured soya milk and blend on a low speed for around 20 seconds. Gradually (if possible) increase the speed to high and blend for another 20-30 seconds.

coconut-carob-orange

Carob (powdered carob beans) is widely used as a chocolate or cocoa substitute because it does not contain caffeine. Carob powder is less soluble than cocoa, and can be a little gritty, so make a smooth paste by mixing it with a little warm water before adding it to the other ingredients.

ingredients

60ml (2fl oz) coconut milk
  (see recipe on page 29)
1 small orange, peeled and
  broken into segments, or
  squeezed and some of the
  skin grated for zest

100ml plain, live yoghurt
  (for recipe, see page 31)
1-2 tsp carob powder,
  made into a smooth paste
  with a little warm water

method

Put the coconut milk, the orange or orange juice and yoghurt into the blender and pour in the carob paste. Blend on a low speed for around 20 seconds. Gradually (if possible) increase the speed to high and blend for another 20-30 seconds. Top with some of the orange zest.

frozen & iced smoothies

Raspberry ripples, strawberries and cream, chocolate milkshakes and ice cream sodas are some of the great pleasures in life, and you don't have to be a kid to enjoy them! In fact, because you can use frozen yoghurt or make your own blender ice cream, you can make a healthy version without sacrificing the flavour.

Cold and creamy or sharp and slushy, these smoothies are a great way to cool off after exercise or on a hot summer's day. (They are just as nice in winter on parched, dry or sore throats!) Consuming nutrients with water sends energy to the muscles while also rehydrating them – those Californian surfers not only knew about waves, they also knew plenty about bodies!

You can turn 'ordinary' fruit smoothies into slushy delights that need a spoon by adding ice, sherbet, frozen juice, frozen yoghurt or milk cubes and of course, ice cream. When you add ice to a smoothie, you are actually adding liquid: the more ice the more dilute the flavours! While ice, sherbet, frozen yoghurt and ice cream will chill a drink, it helps if the other ingredients are also cold. This will keep the smoothie cool all the way through and it won't melt quite so fast!

One regular ice cube is approximately 1½ tablespoons of liquid. So, for 125ml (4fl oz) of liquid, you will need 6 ice cubes. Remember that crushing ice cubes means they will melt pretty quickly, so serve recipes containing crushed ice straight away. You can flavour your ice cubes, make them out of grape, orange or apple juice, strong coffee, mint, tea, or milk of all types (including chocolate, banana or strawberry flavoured milk!). If you are using more than 5 ice cubes in a recipe, it's a good idea to add them to the blender 2 or 3 at a time, but make sure your blender can cope. If it won't crush ice, then you'll have to crush the cubes by hand and add them to the mix.

I've used the word 'scoop' for measures of ice, sherbet and ice cream, which means using a tablespoon and scooping it up rather than one of those ice cream parlour ball scoops. If you need a little more ice in your mix, just add a little more!

You can use ready-made, shop-bought ice cream and sherbet, or you can make your own. There are some recipe suggestions on the following pages which are easy to make in the blender, or you can add an ice cream maker alongside a juicer on your birthday wish list!

Again, with the fruit ingredients, you can use fresh, frozen or canned, or juices. It's up to you! If you are feeling like pushing the boat out, you could even add a dash of a liqueur for a 'boozy smoothy'. There are some wonderful fruit liqueurs available such as Cointreau, Mandarin Napoleon and Grand Marnier which are made with bitter Seville oranges, and the bright green Midori, a melon liqueur! And there are those 'creamy' liqueurs flavoured with coffee, chocolate, mint and berries to tempt adult taste buds. In some recipes I've used grenadine, a fruit syrup made from pomegranates. It gives a wonderful red-pink glow to drinks and is available in a zero-alcohol version, but check the label to make sure! Alternatively, cherry, strawberry or raspberry syrups are tasty alternatives.

sherbet

This sweet but tangy sherbet is made with equal parts sugar and water/fruit juice. I've used the word 'cup' here for the measure: if your cup holds 125ml (3½fl oz) you'll end up with 250ml (½ pint) of sherbet, enough for two good scoops!

ingredients

2 cups sugar

1 cup water

1 cup fruit juice, for example orange, lemon, lime (or lemon-lime), or pink

grapefruit, and some of the grated zest of the fruit

You can also make sherbet with pineapple or 'berry juice', such as blackcurrant, raspberry or cranberry

method

Dissolve 2 cups of sugar in 1 cup of water and simmer gently in a small saucepan for 2-3 minutes. Add 1 cup of citrus fruit juice and the grated zest of the fruit and allow to cool. Then freeze in a suitable container. When ready, the sherbet should have a firm, ice cream texture.

Try layering two or three small scoops of each sherbet in a glass for a variety of flavours. Press the sherbets into the glass on top of each other and chill the glass again in the freezer before serving.

slushy mix

Citrus fruits and berries make terrific slushies, but melons make delicious versions, too. Because they are naturally watery, you won't have to add more water. You can use fresh fruit, squeezed or pulped in the blender. To make 200ml (7fl oz) of juice you'll need about 4 oranges, 1½ grapefruits, 4 lemons, 6 limes, 1 pineapple and 275g (10oz) of berries. If you use melons, 1 honeydew melon or ½ a watermelon will be enough, and leave out the water in the recipe.

ingredients

200ml (7fl oz) or so of juice
100ml (3½fl oz) water

method

Mix the water and the juice in a shallow container and put it in the freezer compartment for about 1 hour. Remove from the freezer and stir the ice crystals around. Place back in the freezer for another half an hour. Remove and stir again. Then its ready to use.

yoghurt slush

Yoghurt is extremely versatile and nutritious. You can use it to replace milk for a slightly thicker mix. Try this frosty fruit delight. You can use frozen peaches, mangoes, apricots, cherries, or any berries you like. Try it too without the sugar for a really sharp taste!

ingredients

85ml (2½fl oz) natural, live yoghurt (see recipe on page 31)
25ml (1fl oz) half-fat evaporated milk
6 frozen strawberries
1 tbsp sugar (or less to taste)
3 frozen skimmed-milk cubes.

method

In the blender, combine the yoghurt, evaporated milk, sugar and 3 of the frozen strawberries for 10 seconds on low speed. Stop and stir the mix, then add the remaining three strawberries. Blend again for 10 seconds. Stop and add the 3 frozen milk cubes and blend, stopping and stirring until the ice is blended thoroughly into the mix. Use straightaway, or pour into a shallow container and freeze for up to 2 hours.

banana blender ice cream

You could just go and buy some ice cream, but it won't taste as nice. Blender ice creams are soft, more 'iced milks', as they don't contain cream. Cream can be used instead of milk, but because it is higher in fat the result will be more solid.

ingredients

85ml (2½fl oz) almond milk (see recipe on page 30)

1 tbsp granulated sugar

1 ripe banana, peeled, chopped and frozen

½ tsp almond extract

4-5 frozen, skimmed-milk ice cubes, crushed if necessary

method

Put the almond milk, frozen banana, sugar, almond extract and skimmed-milk cubes in the blender. Blend for 10 seconds on low speed, stop and stir the mix, then blend again for 10 seconds. Repeat until the ice is blended thoroughly into the mix. Use straight away or pour into a shallow container and freeze for up to 2 hours.

chocolate blender ice cream

You can use carob or cocoa for this and you could even make your milk cubes out of chocolate milk for a richer mix!

ingredients

85ml (2½fl oz) chocolate milk

1 tbsp granulated sugar

1 tbsp carob powder (mixed with a little warm water to make a paste) or unsweetened cocoa powder

6 frozen, skimmed-milk cubes

method

In the blender, combine the milk, granulated sugar, cocoa or carob and 3 of the milk cubes. Blend for 10 seconds on low speed, stop and stir the mix, then add the remaining 3 milk cubes and blend again for 10 seconds. Repeat blending, stopping and stirring until the ice is blended thoroughly into the mix. Use straightaway or pour into a shallow container and freeze for up to 2 hours.

frozen chocolate yoghurt

This simple recipe is a variation on the Chocolate Blender Ice cream: you just replace the milk with plain yoghurt (see recipe on page 31) and use chocolate milk cubes.

ingredients

85ml (2½fl oz) live, natural yoghurt

1 tbsp granulated sugar

1 tbsp carob powder (mixed with a little warm water to make a paste) or unsweetened cocoa powder

6 frozen chocolate milk cubes

method

In the blender, combine the yoghurt, sugar, cocoa or carob and 3 of the chocolate milk cubes. Blend for 10 seconds on low speed, stop and stir the mix, then add the remaining 3 chocolate milk cubes and blend again for 10 seconds. Repeat blending, stopping and stirring until the ice is blended thoroughly into the mix. Use straightaway or pour into a shallow container and freeze for up to 2 hours.

espresso blender ice cream

This is delicious made with coconut milk, but you can substitute plain or almond milk if you like. The coffee flavour is provided by the frozen coffee cubes: just make up enough black coffee, let it cool and then pour into ice cube moulds and freeze.

ingredients

85ml (2½fl oz) milk, coconut or almond milk
1 tbsp granulated sugar
3 frozen espresso coffee cubes
1-2 frozen chocolate milk cubes

method

In the blender, combine the milk, granulated sugar and 3 of the frozen espresso coffee cubes. Blend for 10 seconds on low speed, stop and stir. Then add the chocolate milk cubes and blend again for 10 seconds. Repeat blending, stopping and stirring until the ice is blended thoroughly into the mix. Use straightaway or pour into a shallow container and freeze for up to 2 hours.

strawberry blender ice cream

Evaporated milk in cans is not to be confused with condensed milk – the latter is thicker and much sweeter! You can get evaporated milk in full-fat and half-fat versions. For a really creamy ice cream, use full fat. If you prefer a less rich version, you can use almond milk (see page 30).

ingredients

85ml (2½fl oz) evaporated milk
1 tbsp granulated sugar (or less depending on taste)
3-4 frozen strawberries
3 frozen milk cubes.

method

In the blender, combine the evaporated milk, granulated sugar and the frozen strawberries. Blend for 10 seconds on a low speed. Stop and stir the mix, then add the milk cubes and blend again for 10 seconds. Repeat blending, stopping and stirring until the ice is blended thoroughly into the mix. Use straightaway, or pour into a shallow container and freeze for up to 2 hours.

vanilla blender ice cream

Sometimes, the delicate taste of vanilla is all you need in an ice cream, especially if you want to combine it with other delicate-flavoured fruits like bananas, or even nuts.

ingredients

85ml (2½fl oz) half-fat evaporated milk

1½ tbsp granulated sugar

3-4 frozen strawberries

¼ tsp vanilla extract

5 frozen skimmed-milk cubes

method

In the blender, combine the half-fat evaporated milk, granulated sugar and the vanilla extract with 3 of the milk cubes. Blend for 10 seconds on low speed. Stop and stir the mix, then add the 2 remaining milk cubes and blend again for 10 seconds. Repeat blending, stopping and stirring until the ice is blended thoroughly into the mix. Use straightaway or pour into a shallow container and freeze for up to 2 hours.

choc-cherry

Chocolate and cherry is a really lovely combination. If you are entertaining, you can offer this as a dessert, perhaps with a dash of cherry brandy added!

ingredients

125ml (4fl oz) chilled chocolate milk

125g (4oz) pitted frozen cherries

1 scoop frozen chocolate yoghurt (see recipe on page 183) or chocolate ice cream (or you can use 3 frozen chocolate milk cubes)

method

Place the chocolate milk, frozen yoghurt or ice cream and frozen cherries in the blender. Blend for 10 seconds on low speed. Stop and stir the mix, then blend again for another 10 seconds. Repeat until the mix is smooth.

mocha-mint

Iced coffee is a real refresher in the summer. This mix has a little extra delight in the form of chocolate and mint.

ingredients

125ml (4fl oz) chilled strong, black coffee (decaf if you wish!)

50ml (scant 2fl oz) half-fat evaporated milk

1 tbsp chopped fresh mint leaves

1 tbsp cocoa powder (or carob if you prefer!)

drizzle of honey to sweeten (optional)

6 frozen chocolate milk cubes

pinch ground cinnamon

method

In the blender, combine the chilled black coffee, the half-fat evaporated milk, mint leaves, cocoa powder, the honey (optional) and 3 of the chocolate milk cubes. Blend for 10 seconds on low speed, stop and stir the mix, then add the 3 remaining chocolate milk cubes and blend again for 10 seconds. Repeat blending, stopping and stirring until the ice is blended thoroughly into the mix. Serve immediately with a pinch of cinnamon sprinkled on top and a spoon.

kiwi-lime fizz

Limes have the most gorgeous scent and flavour and they make perfect partners for sweet ripe kiwi fruits, also known as 'Chinese gooseberries'. Kiwis have twice as much Vitamin C as an orange and more fibre than an apple, and they are rich in potassium. Lack of this mineral can lead to high blood pressure, chronic fatigue and depression.

ingredients

1 scoop of lime sherbet (see page 178 for recipe)
1 kiwi fruit, peeled and chopped
1 fresh lime, squeezed

method

Put the lime sherbet in the blender with the chopped kiwi and the lime juice and blend briefly on a low speed.

banana boat

This delightful mix is in fact a *bona fide* cocktail, non-alcoholic, but a cocktail nonetheless!

ingredients

1 small banana, peeled and broken into chunks

75ml (about 3fl oz) chilled milk

25ml (about 1fl oz) coconut cream (see recipe on page 29)

25ml (about 1fl oz) pineapple juice (or 1 thick slice canned fruit)

1 good scoop crushed ice

method

Put the banana, milk, coconut cream and the pineapple juice (or slice of fruit) into the blender and blend together until smooth. Stop and add a good scoop of crushed ice and blend again briefly until mixed. Pour into a glass and garnish with a cherry for a professional finish!

bingo

This fruity blend can be made with ready-made juices or with whole fruits, as you wish, and the fruits can be fresh or canned! It's hard to go wrong with such flavours! Grenadine is a zero (or low) alcohol cordial made from the sweetened juice of the pomegranate *Punta Grenatum* and is ideal as a natural, deep red colourant.

ingredients

25ml (1fl oz) papaya juice, or 1 slice of fruit

25ml (1fl oz) orange juice, or 1/2 orange, squeezed

25ml (1fl oz) pineapple juice, or 1 slice canned fruit

½ lime, squeezed

3-4 strawberries, hulled and halved

25ml (1fl oz) coconut cream (see recipe on page 29)

1 tbsp grenadine

crushed ice

method

Put the papaya juice and pineapple juice (or the slices of fruit) into the blender with the orange juice, lime juice, strawberries, coconut cream and grenadine. Blend until smooth. Stop the blender and add a good scoop of crushed ice and blend briefly until mixed. Pour into a glass and serve with straws.

bora-bora

This inspired drink takes its name from Bora Bora, the tiny South Pacific island in the Society Islands, northwest of Tahiti. Good things often come in small packages!

ingredients

74ml (3fl oz) pineapple juice, or 2-3 slices of fruit, canned
  or fresh
1 tbsp grenadine
½ lime, squeezed
chilled dry ginger ale to top
crushed ice

method

Put the pineapple juice (or fruit) into the blender with the lime juice and grenadine. Blend until smooth. Stop the blender and add a good scoop of crushed ice and blend briefly until mixed. Pour into a glass and top with a little chilled, dry ginger ale and serve with straws.

fruit fairy

If you like cocnut, you'll love this! Coconuts are the largest seeds known to man, and every bit of the palm and fruit is used. This is another 'mocktail', but if you have a dash of creme de banane handy, then you can make a real cocktail!

ingredients

1 small banana, peeled and chopped

25ml (1fl oz) coconut cream (see recipe on page 29)

50ml (2fl oz) pineapple juice, or 2 slices fruit, fresh or canned

2 scoops ready-made vanilla ice cream, or see the recipe on page 186 to make your own

method

Put the banana and the pineapple (or juice) into the blender with the coconut cream and blend until smooth. Stop the blender and add the vanilla ice cream and blend again briefly. Pour into a glass and pop a cherry on top if you like.

fruity fantasy

This is just gorgeous: it's a terrific 'party punch' that's easy to make in volume.

ingredients

75ml (3fl oz) orange juice or one large orange, peeled and broken into segments

50ml (2fl oz) pineapple juice or one thick slice of fruit, chopped

1 kiwi fruit, peeled and chopped

4 strawberries, hulled and halved

2 tbsp melon

2 scoops crushed ice

method

Put the orange and pineapple (or juices) into the blender with the kiwi and strawberries. Add two scoops of melon and blend until smooth. Stop the blender and add 2 good scoops of crushed ice and blend briefly. Pour into a glass and serve with straws. Garnish with some of the fruit, too, if you have some to spare!

hawaiian island surfer

Pineapples are synonymous with the Hawaiian Islands, although they are in fact native to South America. This icy mix of pineapple and coconut cream is great while you wait for the big kahuna!

ingredients

1 big scoop orange sherbet (see recipe on page 178)

50ml (2fl oz) pineapple juice, or 1 thick slice of fruit, chopped

25ml (1fl oz) coconut cream (see recipe on page 29)

method

Put the pineapple (or juice) into the blender with the coconut cream and blend until smooth. Stop the blender and add the orange sherbet and blend again briefly. Pour into a glass and serve with straws.

lemon ice cream soda

The sharp, tangy flavour of lemons is always pleasing on a hot day. You could of course use limes (use 2), or orange juice if you prefer.

ingredients

1 lemon, squeezed

2 good scoops vanilla ice cream, ready-made or see the recipe on page 186

chilled soda water or sparkling mineral water to top

1-2 scoops crushed ice

method

Put the lemon juice into the blender with the vanilla ice cream and blend briefly. Stop the blender and add a scoop (or two) of crushed ice and blend again. Pour into a glass and top with chilled soda or sparkling mineral water and serve with straws.

magic island

This is a really creamy delight that makes a terrific summer dessert. The sharpness of the grapefruit is tempered by the sweetness of the pineapple and coconut.

ingredients

75ml (3fl oz) pineapple juice or 2-3 slices fruit, chopped

25ml (1fl oz) grapefruit juice, or ½ small fruit, squeezed

25ml (1fl oz) coconut cream (see recipe on page 29)

12ml (½fl oz) whipping cream

1 tsp grenadine

2 scoops crushed ice

method

Put the pineapple and grapefruit juices into the blender with the grenadine, coconut cream and the whipping cream and blend until smooth. Stop the blender and add 2 good scoops of crushed ice and blend briefly. Pour into a glass and serve with straws.

mickey mouse

This is a classic: not so much a smoothie as sheer fun!
You don't need the blender for this one, you just 'build'
it in the glass!

ingredients

1 scoop vanilla ice cream, ready-made or see recipe on
   page 186

25ml (1fl oz) whipped cream

cold cola to top

2 cherries

grated chocolate

method

Whip the cream until stiff. Put the vanilla ice cream into the glass
and pour on the cola. Top with the whipped cream and pop the
cherries on top and sprinkle a little grated chocolate on top.
Serve with straws and maybe a spoon too!

passion cooler

Passion fruit has a glorious flavour, although many people are put off by the seeds. You can strain the fruit through a sieve if you want a seedless version, or use passion fruit juice.

ingredients

50ml (2fl oz) pineapple juice, or 2 sliced fruit, chopped
50ml (2fl oz) mango juice, or half a mango, chopped
25ml (1fl oz) or ½ orange, squeezed
25ml (1fl oz) passion fruit juice or 1 passion fruit
½ banana, peeled and chopped
crushed ice

method

Put the banana, the orange juice, the mango and pineapple juice (or fruit) into the blender with the passion fruit (or juice) and blend until smooth. Stop the blender and add a good scoop of crushed ice and blend again. Pour into a glass and serve immediately.

shirley's sister

The Shirley Temple was a non-alcoholic cocktail devised for the Hollywood child-star. It was simply a dash of grenadine in lemon-lime soda or ginger ale. Her 'sister' is similar, but with the added luxury of ice cream and melted chocolate!

ingredients

15ml/1 tbsp grenadine

1 big scoop strawberry ice cream, ready-made or see recipe on page 185

1-2 squares of chocolate, melted

75ml (3fl oz) chilled lemonade

broken ice cubes

1 strawberry, for garnish

method

Melt the chocolate, or cheat and use chocolate syrup! Put some broken ice cubes into a tall glass to fill it half full. Pour in the grenadine and add the chilled lemonade. Fill up the glass by floating the strawberry ice cream on top and drizzle on the melted chocolate. Pop a strawberry on the side of the glass and serve with straws.

strawberry kiss

An irresistible strawberry-and-cream-delight. Like pineapple, strawberries contain bromelain that 'digests' protein. They are also reputed to be a 'cure' for rheumatism and arthritis, as they expel uric acid from the body.

ingredients

6-8 strawberries, hulled and halved
50ml (2fl oz) pineapple juice, or 1 slice of fruit, chopped
½ lemon, squeezed
12ml (½fl oz) whipping cream
2 scoops crushed ice

method

Put the strawberries in the blender with the pineapple (or juice) and the lemon juice. Blend until smooth. Add the whipping cream and the crushed ice and blend again until mixed. Pour into a glass and serve immediately.

strawberry split

A really fruity 'slushy'! The combination of strawberries, pineapple and apple juice make for a deliciously refreshing drink. If you prefer, you can substitute sparkling mineral water for the lemonade.

ingredients

6-8 strawberries, hulled and halved
25ml (1fl oz) pineapple juice, or 1 tbsp of crushed fruit
25ml (1fl oz) apple juice
½ lime, squeezed
chilled lemonade
crushed ice

method

Put the strawberries and pineapple (or pineapple juice) into the blender along with the apple juice and the lime juice and blend until smooth. Stop the blender and add a good scoop or two of crushed ice and blend again. Pour into a tall glass and top with chilled lemonade and serve with straws.

summer rain

Cooling and refreshing, like a summer shower. When you pop a raspberry in your mouth you are, in fact, eating about 80 single fruits as raspberries are clusters of little fruits called druplets.

ingredients

2 scoops orange sherbet (see recipe on page 178)

10 raspberries, fresh, frozen or canned

25ml (1fl oz) pineapple juice, or 1 tbsp chopped fruit

½ pink grapefruit, squeezed

1 dash of chilled lemonade

crushed ice

method

Put the raspberries into the blender with the pineapple (or juice) and purée until smooth. Squeeze in the grapefruit juice and add the orange sherbet. Blend until smooth. Add 2 scoops of crushed ice and blend again briefly. Pour into a tall glass and add the splash of chilled lemonade. Serve immediately with straws.

summer soda

This has a lovely citrus-vanilla flavour. If you like your mix a little less sweet, just omit the sugar. You can use ready-made ice cream or check out the recipe on page 186 to make your own.

ingredients

25ml (1fl oz) orange juice, or ½ orange squeezed
25ml (1fl oz) grapefruit juice, ½ small grapefruit, squeezed
½ lemon, squeezed
1 tsp sugar
1 scoop vanilla ice cream
75ml (3fl oz) chilled soda or mineral water
broken ice

method

Dissolve the sugar in the juices and add with the soda or mineral water, to a tall glass a quarter filled with broken ice. Float the ice cream on the top and add some straws and a spoon.

tail feathers

Another classic 'mocktail', this time based on the Highball, a long drink first devised by New York bartender, Patrick Duffy in 1895. The chopped mint dispersed throughout the drink is really refreshing. If you prefer, you can substitute mineral water for the ginger ale.

ingredients

125ml (4fl oz) orange juice, or 3 oranges squeezed

2 limes, squeezed

2-3 leaves of fresh mint, chopped

chilled ginger ale to top

crushed ice

method

Mix the orange juice with the lime juice and chopped mint. Half fill a glass with plenty of crushed ice and pour over the fruit mix. Top with a little chilled ginger ale and decorate with a sprig of mint.

grenadine frappé

Very simple, but very refreshing. Grenadine is made from the juice of pomegranates and gives mixed drinks a gorgeous pink colour as well as a fruity sweetness. Make sure your grenadine is zero-alcohol if you don't want a boozy blend!

ingredients

1 scoop lemon sherbet (see recipe on page 178)

1 lime, squeezed

1 tbsp grenadine

slice of lime and a sprig of mint to garnish

method

Mix the grenadine and lime juice together. Put the sherbet into a glass and pour the juice mix over the top. Decorate with the lime slice and the mint sprig.

clementine & lemon fizz

This is like a lovely melting ice-lolly or popsicle, with a little fizz! You can use clementines, mandarins or satsumas for this, or try a tangelo (a hybrid of a mandarin, grapefruit and pommelo) or a tangor (a hybrid of mandarins and oranges).

ingredients

2 scoops lemon sherbet (see recipe on page 178)
4 clementines (or mandarins or satsumas), squeezed

method

Put the sherbet into the blender and squeeze the juice of the clementines over it. Blend until smooth and frothy. Serve immediately with a straw. You can, if you wish, peel the clementines and purée them first in the blender, then add the sherbet and blend together.

avalanche

This is another very simple, but wonderfully refreshing drink for hot days. You can use lemon or lime sorbet for this – the recipe is on page 178. For a 'boozy smoothie', you could even add a splash of gin.

ingredients

1 scoop lemon sherbet (see recipe on page 178)

chilled bitter lemon

2-3 slices of lime

crushed ice

method

Fill a tall glass half full with crushed ice, slipping two of the lime slices into the glass as well. Pop the scoop of lemon sherbet on top. Top up with a little chilled bitter lemon and decorate with the last lime slice.

almond coffee

For this recipe you can use orgeat, a widely available almond flavoured syrup, or simply a dash of almond essence. Both will make a lovely, long creamy drink with coffee for a hot summer's day.

ingredients

2 scoops ice cream, for vanilla or banana blender ice cream, see recipes on pages 186 and 181
1 tablespoon orgeat (almond syrup) or ½ tsp almond essence
100ml (3½fl oz) strong, cold coffee
whipped cream
almond flakes or chopped almonds

method

Make the coffee and allow to chill. When ready, pour in the orgeat or almond essence and stir. Put the ice cream into the glass and pour on the coffee mix. Heap some whipped cream on top and sprinkle almond flakes or chopped nuts on top.

raspberry ripple

A firm favourite: raspberries have the most lovely taste, but you can ripple with any berry! Raspberries are renowned for their high Vitamin C content and this ripple will provide you with around 75% of your daily needs!

ingredients

125g (4oz) raspberries, fresh, frozen or canned
2 scoops vanilla ice cream (see recipe on page 186)

method

Put the raspberries into the blender with one scoop of ice cream and blend together. Put the second scoop of ice cream into a glass and pour the creamy mix over the top.

pineapple & orange slushy

Another very simple mix. Follow the quantities given for the slushy mix on page 179, then add the pineapple juice and you will end up with two good-sized servings of delicious slushy.

ingredients

For 2 servings:

orange slushy mix (see recipe on page 179)

200ml (about 7fl oz) pineapple juice

method

Divide the slushy mix between two glasses and drizzle the pineapple juice over the top.

strawberry peach

This drink has all the flavours of a perfect summer day in the country. Using the quantities given for the slushy mix (see page 179), this recipe will yield 2 medium-sized servings. You can use shop-bought peach 'nectar' if you like, or for a really thick slushy, peel, quarter and purée the peaches in the blender, or use frozen peaches for a really icy slushy!

ingredients

For 2 servings:

strawberry slushy mix (see page 179)

200ml (7fl oz) peach nectar, or 3 peaches, peeled and puréed, in the blender, or use frozen peaches

method

Divide the slushy mix between two glasses and pour the peach nectar on top. If using fresh or frozen peaches, blend them in the blender and spoon into the glass with the slushy in alternate layers!

frozen melon

Melons are watery fruits and therefore really refreshing. Using the quantities given for the slushy mix (see page 179) this will serve two thirsty people. Cantaloupe melons have a lovely golden-coloured flesh and the fruit is full of carotenoids which are believed to inhibit the growth of cancer cells.

ingredients

For 2 servings:

orange slushy mix (see page 179)

½ cantaloupe melon, de-seeded and chopped

method

Put the melon into the blender and blend until smooth. Divide the orange slushy mix between two glasses and pour the melon juice over the top.

peach slushy

This works best if both the peaches and the yoghurt are frozen: 6 frozen yoghurt cubes will give you the equivalent of about 125ml (4fl oz) of yoghurt, so you'll need about 8 cubes for this recipe. You can use flavoured yoghurt or, if you prefer, make your own live natural yoghurt using the recipe on page 31.

ingredients

2 peaches, peeled, quartered and frozen

8 frozen yoghurt cubes, any flavour you like, or plain live yoghurt

method

Put the frozen peaches into the blender with 2 or 3 frozen yoghurt cubes and blend until smooth. Stop the blender, stir the mix, add 3 more yoghurt cubes and blend again. Stop, stir and add the remaining yoghurt cubes and blend again. Pour into a glass and serve immediately.

orange blossom

A delicious, thick, smooth and very fragrant drink. Again, use any plain (unflavoured) yoghurt, shop-bought or home-made (see recipe on page 31) frozen in ice cube trays. For this recipe, you'll need about 8 frozen yoghurt cubes.

ingredients

1 orange, peeled and broken into segments

1 nectarine, peeled and chopped

8 frozen yoghurt cubes

method

Put the orange and the nectarine into the blender and blend until smooth. Stop the blender and add 3 yoghurt cubes and blend again. Stop, stir the mix and add 3 more yoghurt cubes and blend again briefly. Stop, stir and add the final cubes and blend again. Pour into a glass and serve straightaway.

green snow

The vivid colour may be a little strange, but melon and kiwi combine in the most delicious way. Using the quantities given for the slushy mix on page 179, this recipe will serve two. For a truly adult treat, add a splash of the bright-green melon liqueur Midori into the mix!

ingredients

For two servings:
melon slushy mix (see page 179)
3 kiwi fruits, peeled and chopped.

method

Peel and chop the kiwis and combine them in the blender until smooth. Add the slushy mix and stir gently. (At this stage you can add the Midori, 25ml/1fl oz will be enough for two!). Divide the mix between two glasses and serve.

frozen barbie

Yes it's pink! Use the slushy mix recipe on page 179 and this recipe will serve two 'living dolls'. Watermelon are in fact botanically unrelated to 'true' melons (which include pumpkins and cucumbers). Nevertheless there are few tastier – or more refreshing – fruits.

ingredients

For two servings:

strawberry slushy mix (see page 179)

½ watermelon, de-seeded and chopped

method

Scoop the flesh out of the watermelon and pass it through a sieve to separate the seeds, or just pick them out one by one, and purée the flesh in the blender. Add the slushy mix and stir gently, then divide between two glasses.

double chocolate milkshake

The Aztecs prized cocoa beans so highly they were used as currency. One of the major ingredients of chocolate is theobromine, a stimulating chemical similar to caffeine but much gentler. This is thought to release the natural 'feel-good' chemicals in the brain, the endorphins, which give rise to romantic thoughts!

ingredients

40g (about 1½oz) dark chocolate - look for a high cocoa content!
2 scoops chocolate ice cream (see recipe on page 182 to make your own)
200ml (7fl oz) cold milk

method

Melt the chocolate, using a small bowl sitting in a larger bowl of hot water. Put the ice cream into the blender, and pour in half of the milk. Mix the remaining milk with the melted chocolate, then pour it into the blender. Blend until the mix is dark and frothy. Serve immediately.?

death by chocolate

To die for! There's slightly more chocolate in this recipe and instead of ice cream, it uses whole (full-fat) milk. For a really rich and creamy smoothie, try using Guernsey or Jersey milk from the Channel Islands!

ingredients

75g (2½oz) dark chocolate, go for quality chocolate with a high cocoa content

175ml (6fl oz) chilled whole (full-fat) milk

2 ice cubes
shaved/grated chocolate

method

Break the chocolate into pieces and place in a bowl set over a larger bowl of hot water. Add 4 tablespoons/60ml of the milk and melt the chocolate, stirring once or twice with a wooden spoon. When melted, remove the bowl from the heat, pour the remaining milk into the chocolate mix and stir to combine. Pour the mix into the blender with 2 ice cubes and blend until frothy. Pour into a glass and grate/shave a little extra chocolate on top.

coconut & passion fruit ice

Coconut and passion fruit is a truly tropical taste. If you use fresh coconut, you'll need about 125g (5oz). Drain off the milk and shred the flesh with a grater (you can freeze any leftovers), and follow the recipe below.

ingredients

75ml/5 tbsp unsweetened, dried, shredded coconut

125ml (4fl oz) boiling water

½ tsp vanilla essence

1 passion fruit, halved with flesh scooped out

1 good scoop crushed ice

20ml/2 tbsp double cream

method

In the blender, combine the boiling water, vanilla essence and the shredded coconut. Blend on a low speed for around 20 seconds. Gradually (if possible) increase the speed to high and blend for another 20-30 seconds. Let it cool, then cover and chill. When very cold, put the crushed ice into the blender and pour on the coconut mix and the double cream. Blend briefly to combine. Pour the mix into a tall glass and spoon the passion fruit on top. Serve immediately.

strawberry trifle

The classic flavours of trifle. The sherry, however, is optional!

ingredients

½ apple, cored and chopped

100g (3½oz) strawberries, hulled and halved

½ tsp caster sugar

1 tbsp sherry (optional)

40ml/4 tbsp double cream

flaked almonds

1 large scoop vanilla or strawberry ice cream (see recipes on pages 185-6)

method

Chop the apple and divide the strawberries into two piles. Put the apples and half of the strawberries in the blender and blend on a low speed for around 20 seconds. Gradually (if possible) increase the speed to high and blend for another 20-30 seconds. Add the sugar and the sherry and blend briefly again. Chill until ready to serve. Whip the cream until it just holds its shape. Put the remaining strawberries into a glass and sprinkle with a few nuts. Put a scoop of ice cream on top and then pour over the strawberry and apple mix and finish with the whipped cream.

rum & raisin shake

People have been drying fruit in the sun for thousands of years: the Romans in particular included raisins in their medicinal recipes. All the natural benefits of the grape are concentrated into raisins, making them a wonderful store of instant energy and a delicious and nutritious treat.

ingredients

40g (about 1½oz) raisins, if they are a little dry, soak them in the rum

1 tbsp dark rum

125ml (¼ pint) whole (full-fat) milk

2 good scoops vanilla ice cream (see recipe on page 186)

method

Put the raisins, rum and a splash of milk into the blender and blend for about 1 minute or so until the raisins are finely chopped. Put 1 scoop of ice cream into a glass and place the second scoop in the blender along with the remaining milk. Blend until smooth and creamy. Pour the milk mix over the ice cream and serve immediately with a spoon.

mango, ginger & grapefruit slushy

A really creamy, thick mix that, despite the icy appearance, is, thanks to the volatile oils in the ginger, quite warming! The mango alone will provide you with 50% of your daily Vitamin C requirements and 25% of your Vitamin E and A needs.

ingredients

½ mango, fresh or canned
2 pink grapefruits, peeled and broken into segments
1 slice of ginger, about 1cm/½in, peeled and chopped
crushed ice

method

Put the mango, grapefruit and ginger in the blender and blend until smooth. Stop the machine and add either 6 ice cubes, 3 at a time, blending and stirring after each, or 2 scoops of crushed ice and blend briefly. Pour into a glass and serve immediately.

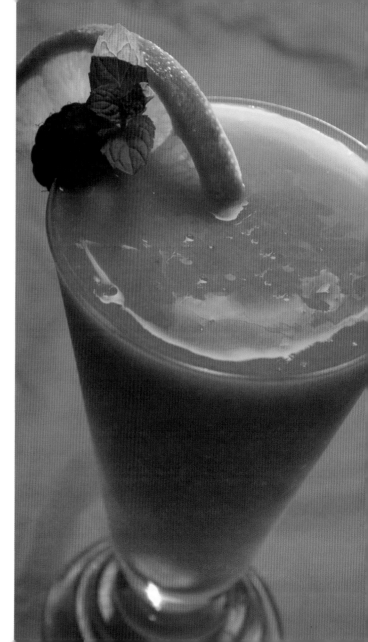

frosted fruits of the forest

This is a delicious smoothie, making great use of the flavours of mixed summer fruits. You can use your favourite berry fruits in any proportion in this smoothie.

ingredients

125g (4oz) frozen mixed berries

100ml (3½fl oz) plain, live yoghurt (see recipe on page 31)

1 tbsp double cream

1 tsp caster sugar, or a drizzle of honey, to taste

method

Take the frozen berries straight from the freezer and put them into the blender. Blend until crushed and smooth. Add the yoghurt and the cream and the sugar/honey. Blend again until the mix is thick and smooth. Taste and adjust for sweetness and serve straightaway.

pistachio shake

Sometimes called 'green almonds', pistachios have been eaten for well over 4,000 years. They grow in clusters on trees that are related to the tropical cashew and the sumac, and when ripe are beaten off the trees with sticks. They are so delicious, you often have to use a stick to stop people from eating them! They are fairly high in protein but are also 50% fat, and most is unsaturated.

ingredients

25g (about 1oz) shelled,
    unsalted pistachio nuts
boiling water

8 frozen yoghurt cubes
    (for the recipe to make your
    own yoghurt, see page 31)

method

Put the pistachios in a heat-proof bowl and cover with boiling water. Leave them to stand for a few minutes, then drain. Rub the nuts between layers of kitchen paper to loosen the skins. Put the nuts into the blender and add 2 of the frozen yoghurt cubes and blend. Stop and stir the mix and then add 2 more yoghurt cubes. Repeat until all the yoghurt cubes are blended and the nuts well mixed.

rosemary & ginger smoothie

This fragrant ice cream smoothie has a ginger nut biscuit crumbled into the mix, or you could use a ratafia or amaretti biscuit if you prefer an almond taste!

ingredients

2 long sprigs of fresh rosemary

250ml (about ½ pint) whole (full-fat) milk

2-3 ginger biscuits, crumbled, (set a little aside for garnish)

1 large scoop vanilla ice cream (see recipe on page 186)

1 small sprig of rosemary to decorate

method

Put the rosemary in a small pan, add about one-third of the milk and heat very gently until it begins to boil. Remove the pan from the heat and leave to cool. Remove the rosemary leaves and pour the slightly warm milk into the blender. Add the crumbled ginger biscuits and blend until smooth and creamy. Add the rest of the milk and blend thoroughly. Put the scoop of vanilla ice cream into the blender with the milk mix and combine. Serve with a sprinkle of crumbled ginger biscuit and the rosemary on top.

crème de menthe

Not the alcoholic liqueur, but a minty iced yoghurt smoothie – although you could add a dash if you wish. Mint is not only an excellent digestive aid, it also helps to relieve headaches, especially those caused by stress, so this is a terrific way to chill out!

ingredients

1 small bunch of mint, about 8 leaves, chopped finely
100ml (3½fl oz) yoghurt (for the recipe to make your own yoghurt, see page 31)
crushed ice

method

Chop the mint finely, reserving a sprig for garnish. Put the yoghurt into the blender and sprinkle in the chopped mint. Blend until smooth and the mint is well distributed. If it is a little too thick, add a dash of cold milk and blend again. Put some crushed ice into a glass and pour over the yoghurt mix. Pop a sprig of mint on top and serve straightaway.

pear pastis

Pastis, from the French word for 'mixture', is a liquorice-flavoured liquor which, when mixed with water, becomes cloudy. While this version doesn't have the alcohol content, it does look a little like a pastis and it does make use of star anise for the flavour!

ingredients

3 tbsp water

3-4 star anise, crushed

½ tbsp caster sugar

2 pears, fresh (peeled and cored) or canned, chopped

chilled sparkling mineral water

method

Crush the star anise and place in a small saucepan. Add the sugar and 3 tablespoons of water and bring to the boil. Stirring the mix, let it bubble for about 2 minutes. Remove from the heat and allow to stand for about 10 minutes. Chop the pear flesh, place in the blender and blend until smooth. Strain the star anise liquor through a fine sieve and pour it into the pear mix. Stir well. Put the pear mix into a tall glass and top with sparkling chilled mineral water and serve immediately.

cardamom, passion fruit & orange crush

Cardamom is a herb that is very useful in treating digestive problems and it cleanses and fragrances the mouth.

ingredients

½ tbsp cardamom pods

½ tbsp caster sugar

3 tbsp water

1 passion fruit, halved with the flesh scooped out

2 oranges, peeled and broken into segments

3-4 ice cubes

method

Crush the cardamom pods and place in a small pan with the sugar. Stir in 3 tablespoons of water and simmer on a low heat for 5 minutes. Cool and strain through a fine sieve. Put the fruit into the blender and blend on a low speed for around 20 seconds. Add the herb 'syrup' and 2 ice cubes and blend, then add the remaining cubes. Blend again briefly and then pour into a tall glass.

mango & lemon crush

A really refreshing drink which you can make longer with some mineral water, if you like, and some ice. The sweetness of the mango is perfectly offset by the sharpness of the lemon juice.

ingredients

½ mango, fresh or canned, chopped
½ lemon, squeezed
8 frozen yogurt cubes (for yoghurt recipe, see page 31)

method

Chop the mango and place in the blender. Squeeze on the lemon juice. Blend briefly with 3 of the yoghurt cubes. Stop and stir the mix then add 3 more yoghurt cubes. Blend again, then stop, stir, add the 2 remaining cubes and blend briefly.

granizado de cassis

Cassis is the French for blackcurrants, from which the liqueur crème de cassis is made. You can use this, or if you prefer a non-alcoholic version, use a blackcurrant cordial instead.

ingredients

20ml (about ¼fl oz) blackcurrant cordial or crème de cassis
½ orange, squeezed
chilled soda or mineral water
crushed ice

method

Put the blackcurrant cordial into a glass and mix in the orange juice. Fill the glass a quarter full with crushed ice and top with a dash or two of chilled soda or mineral water.

You can also make a Granadizo de Limon, a lime version of this drink: use *Rose's* Lime Juice and the squeezed juice of half a fresh lime in place of the cassis/blackcurrant.

blushing virgin

'Virgins' are the generic name for non-alcoholic cocktails. This drink gets its name from the 'blush' of ruby colour from blood oranges that are the product of Spain and Italy. For thousands of years, oranges have been valued for their health-giving properties. Even Jupiter is said to have given his bride, Juno, an orange on their wedding day!

ingredients

2 blood oranges, squeezed
2 scoops vanilla ice cream (see recipe on page 186)
a dash of chilled soda or mineral water

method

Squeeze the juice from the blood oranges. Put the ice cream into a tall glass and pour the orange juice over the top. Add a dash of chilled soda or mineral water and stir briefly.

pear & cinnamon milkshake

A very fruity drink that's so good you could drink it every day. The Italian grand duke, Cosimo III de Medici, had a passion for pears: he served 209 different varieties at his table one year!

ingredients

6 frozen milk cubes
1 tbsp single cream
1 pear, fresh or canned
2-3 drops vanilla essence
1 tsp lemon juice
½ tsp ground cinnamon

method

Put the pear, vanilla essence, lemon juice, cream and 3 of the frozen milk cubes in the blender with the ground cinnamon. Blend until smooth, then stop and stir the mix, add the remaining milk cubes and blend again.

peach melba
in a glass

The original 'Peach Melba' was created by the great French chef Escoffier for the Australian soprano Dame Nellie Melba. Both, no doubt, would have approved of this version.

ingredients

60g (about 2½oz) raspberries, fresh, frozen or canned

1 peach, fresh or canned

1 tsp sugar

100ml (3½fl oz) chilled, whole (full-fat milk)

1 tbsp single cream

1 scoop vanilla ice cream (see recipe on page 186)

method

Purée the raspberries in the blender, add the sugar and blend again. Put the raspberry purée into the bottom of a tall glass. Purée the peach in the blender and add the milk, cream and vanilla ice cream. Blend together briefly and pour gently into the glass on top of the raspberries.

virgin raspberry daiquiri

This recipe calls for raspberry syrup which is widely available in supermarkets. Look for it next to the ice cream chests! If you don't have any to hand, you can use half a tablespoon of the syrup from a can of raspberries instead!

ingredients

60g (about 2½oz) raspberries, fresh, frozen or canned
50ml (about 2fl oz) pineapple juice, or 1 slice canned fruit
½ lemon, squeezed
1 tsp caster sugar
½ tbsp raspberry syrup
2 scoops crushed ice

method

Put the raspberries and the pineapple into the blender and blend until smooth. Add the lemon juice, the sugar and the raspberry syrup and blend again. Put 2 scoops of crushed ice in the blender and stir the mix together. Pour into a glass and garnish with a raspberry or two!

virgin snowball

A true snowball contains advocaat, a brandy-and-egg liqueur made in Holland. This vanilla-flavoured confection is equally nice!

ingredients

1 apple, peeled, cored and chopped

2-3 drops vanilla essence

8 frozen plain yoghurt ice cubes (see page 31 for recipe)

method

Put the apple into the blender and purée it until smooth. Add the vanilla essence and 3 of the frozen yoghurt cubes. Blend, then stop and stir, then add 3 more frozen yoghurt cubes. Blend again then stop, stir and add the remaining cubes and blend again briefly. Serve immediately.

muddy snowball

This is a great-tasting snowball, especially if you are fond of chocolate. You can use frozen chocolate yoghurt or milk cubes, or chocolate ice cream, if you prefer. Either way, the combination with apple is truly inspired!

ingredients

1 apple, peeled, cored and chopped

2-3 drops vanilla essence

8 frozen chocolate yoghurt or milk cubes, or 1 good scoop of chocolate ice

grated chocolate

method

Put the apple into the blender and purée it until smooth. Add the vanilla essence and 3 of the frozen yoghurt/milk cubes (or if using, the ice cream) and blend briefly until mixed. Blend then stop and stir, then add 3 more frozen yoghurt cubes. Blend again then stop, stir and add the remaining cubes and blend again briefly. Serve immediately – with a little grated chocolate on top!

bibliography:

Friedrich Bohlmann **Energy Drinks** *Gaia Books, 1999*

Pat Crocker **The Smoothies Bible** *Robert Rose, 2003*

Robert Cross **The Classic 1000 Cocktail Recipes** *Foulsham, 1996*

Rose Elliot and Carlo de Paoli **Kitchen Pharmacy** *Orion, 1991*

Joanna Farrow **Smooth and Juicy** *Aquamarine, 2003*

Kirsten Hartvig **Eat For Immunity** *Duncan Baird, 2002*

Kirsten Hartvig and Nick Rowley **Energy Juices** *Duncan Baird, 2001*

Patrick Holford **The Optimum Nutrition** *Bible Piatkus, 1997*

Leslie Kenton **The Raw Energy Bible** *Vermillion, 1998*

Anne McIntyre **Healing Drinks** *Gaia Books, 1999*

Anne McIntyre **Herbs for Common Ailments** *Gaia Books, 1999*

Judith Millidge **The Handbook of Smoothies and Juicing** *Silverdale Books, 2003*

Suzanne Olivier and Joanna Farrow **Juices and Smoothies** *Anness, 2003*

Evelyn Roehl **Whole Food Facts** *Healing Arts Press, 1996*

Jane Sen **The Healing Foods Cookbook** *Thorsons, 1996*

Nigel Slater **Thirst** *Fourth Estate, 2002*

Michael van Straten **Foods for Mind and Body** *Thorsons, 1997*

Michael van Straten **Superjuice** *Mitchell Beazley, 1999*

Caroline Wheater **Juicing For Health** *Thorsons, 1993*

Rebecca Wood **The Whole Foods Encyclopedia** *Prentice Hall, 1988*

Charmaine Yabsley and Amanada Cross **Miracle Juices** *Hamlyn, 2001*

index

credits

Paul for pictures
Diana and Vic for 'taste testing'

about the author

Maria Costantino was born in Chicago, Illinois, and grew up in the US before moving to Britain. As well as lecturing at a number of universities in London and the southeast of England, she is the author of several books including the Cocktail Handbook, the Handbook of Energy Drinks and the Detox Handbook. .